TABLE OF CONTENTS

If My Inside Was My Outside

Then no one would know   In a glance
                                                     In a first look
                                         What I was
                                         Or more important
                                                            who I was

If my inside was my outside

Then you wouldn't
    judge me   What I think What I feel
    label me   What I love What I hate
    make assumptions   What movies I like to watch
                                         What food I like to eat
                                         What music I like to listen to
                                         What language I like to speak
Without first
    asking me questions
And you would want to ask me questions
    If my inside was my outside
    Because it would be the only way
                                         To know

If my inside was my outside

Then the first thing   My color
you'd see   My breasts
wouldn't be   My walk
                                            My hair
                              My heritage
                                   My talk

Diversity and Young Adolescents
More Than Color

by

Elizabeth D. Dore

National Middle School Association
Westerville, Ohio

National Middle School Association
4151 Executive Parkway, Suite 300
Westerville, Ohio 43081
Telephone (800) 528-NMSA
web: www.nmsa.org

Copyright ©2004 by National Middle School Association.

Printed in the United States of America.

Sue Swaim, Executive Director
Jeff Ward, Deputy Executive Director
April Tibbles, Director of Publications
Edward Brazee, Editor, Professional Publications
John Lounsbury, Consulting Editor, Professional Publications
Mary Mitchell, Designer and Editorial Assistant
Mark Shumaker, Cover Design
Dawn Williams, Production Specialist
Marcia Meade-Hurst, Senior Publications Representative

Library of Congress Cataloging-in-Publication Data
Dore, Elizabeth D., date-
   Diversity and young adolescents: more than color/by Elizabeth D. Dore
     p. cm.
   Includes bibliographical references.
   ISBN 1-56090-144-6 (pbk.)
   1. Teenagers--United States--Social conditions. 2. Social interaction in
adolescence--United States. 3. Adolescence--United States. 4. Minority
teenagers--United States. 5. Multiculturalism. I. Title.

HQ796b.D626 2004
305.235'089--dc22   2004040250

If my inside was my outside

Then you couldn't   I am here to get married
make   I can't manage on my own
mistaken assumptions   I am here on a scholarship
I am sensitive by nature
I have no deep feelings
I shouldn't be called on in class
You better lock your doors
I'll understand and tolerate
your jokes
I have money and you can't
have any
I'll probably get AIDS
I only sit with people like me
I use my body as my resumé

If my inside was my outside

Then I wouldn't be afraid
To walk by myself alone
To sit with you in the café
To raise my hand in class
To let you know who I am
To get to parties where I am outnumbered
To see a teacher after class
To investigate my own life instead of
trying to copy yours

If my inside was my outside

Then you really wouldn't know
You'd have to get to know me first

You'd have to say hello

And after you got to know me
You might still find I'm a jerk
But you couldn't just assume it

It would take a little work

And you might find out
I'm beautiful

> You might find that in the end
> You'll get something you hadn't counted on
> You'll get yourself a friend

We all know there's harassment
    It takes on many forms
  It happens in the classroom
    In organizations
    In the dorms

But if my inside was my outside

> We could change this reality
> Because you'd have to forget
>   all the stereotypes
> And just concentrate on me

Reprinted with permission from Real World Productions (612.824.7353)

Foreword

Aren't all young adolescents diverse? Is it redundant to talk about the diversity in and among middle school students? After all, young adolescents develop tremendously in several critical areas between the ages of 10 and 15, most visibly in their physical development, but as importantly in their social, emotional, and intellectual development. This diversity is the middle school story, but it extends far beyond these characteristics.

Young adolescents are also diverse in many other ways, some are obvious, such as race, ethnicity, and socioeconomic status, and some less obvious but equally powerful ways including family structure, gender bias, and a variety of exceptionalities. In *Diversity and Young Adolescents: More Than Color*, Elizabeth Dore explores the nature of diversity in young adolescents and its implications for schools and teachers in their classrooms. This down-to-earth examination of the factors that make young adolescents diverse is written in an easy to understand style, drawing on the significant experiences of Dr. Dore as teacher and university professor in several states.

In addition to background information on the various types of diversity presented at the end of each section, the author provides a number of useful strategies for classroom teachers as they respond to the unique needs of all students. These strategies provide specific activities, possible assignments, and resources for each of the major concepts presented. The savvy teacher will also recognize that many of the strategies are appropriate and engaging for students—as well as other teachers. An excellent annotated bibliography of professional resources, organized by category, is available at the end of the book. This will be used by many teachers to identify outstanding trade books for their students.

In life there are the doers, the people who always get things done, and the talkers who recognize what needs to be done but never seem to get around to doing it. Betty Dore has always been a doer. She cuts through the details of life and goes directly for what needs to be done. Just a few years ago, this educator was a classroom teacher in Gardiner, Maine, fine-tuning her classroom for her students and helping to make her school a functioning middle school. All the while she was also completing a master's degree in middle level education; then, without losing a beat she was off to Colorado where she completed a middle level doctoral program at the University of Northern Colorado.

Betty's years as a classroom teacher and continuing work with her undergraduate students have prepared her well for writing this book. She knows a great deal about young adolescents, and she has worked with a variety of middle level students in diverse settings over the years. These experiences with real kids are reflected throughout this book.

Yes, all middle school students are diverse—even those who do not appear to be. Read this book, savor it, and use the excellent ideas presented here as you continue to work with this special population we call young adolescents.

Edward N. Brazee
Orono, Maine

Introduction

Classroom teachers today are faced with a multitude of diverse conditions. No longer can they expect to face a group of children who are homogeneous in any way. Rather, they must be prepared to understand their students who may reflect a variety of cultures, traditions, and backgrounds. Every classroom will challenge teachers with these very interesting and diverse groups of youngsters. This book will be a stepping-stone to that understanding. It is intended as a supplement to other texts in middle school teacher preparation courses, but it may also be used by veteran classroom teachers looking for effective strategies to reach new and diverse classroom populations. It is a compilation of ideas old and new, concepts from middle school gurus, as well as from newcomers. Pre-service teachers, first-year teachers, and veteran teachers will find it useful in helping to develop lesson plans and in providing information about diverse classroom settings.

This is also a book for parents, guardians, and anyone interested in young adolescents. It is for anyone confused about their thoughts or actions, and for those who want to understand and find ways to help 10 to 15-year-olds become successful young adults.

In its position paper on diversity, National Middle School Association (n.d.) says it this way:

- The success of our nation and humankind itself depends on our collective ability to have mutual respect and appreciation of others.

- Schools must model a community that is based on justice and the celebration of similarities and differences among its members.

- Organizations must encourage diversity as they design policies and standards.

- Organizations are strengthened by continued involvement of under-represented populations that may vary over time. (www.nmsa.org)

Webster's *Ninth New Collegiate Dictionary* (1993) describes diversity as "(1) the condition of being different, variety; (2) an instance or a point of difference." When one thinks of middle school and middle school students, "a condition of being different" certainly comes to mind. There are, however, a multitude of "differences." Four categories, *physical, intellectual, emotional,* and *social,* are often used when describing young adolescents; and these terms may be used to discuss diversity in middle schools and middle school students.

Included in *physical diversity* are physical exceptionalities, stereotyping, racial, gender, and geographic differences. Learning styles and abilities, family expectations, and language (body language, cultural differences, voice, geographical accents, and word or phrase connotations—based on geographical localities) are all included in *intellectual differences. Emotional characteristics* include values, ethnicity, and religious preferences. Finally, *social diversity* includes sexual orientation, socioeconomic status, students at risk, family makeup such as one parent male, one parent female, divorce, death, adoption, and cultural issues.

Miller-Lachmann and Taylor (1995) emphatically state the importance of learning to get along with all people:

> The realities faced by all members of this global society mandate that we learn how to live and work together. At stake are the progress and survival of all inhabitants of the earth. Through knowledge and appreciation of our different cultures and by valuing every group's contributions to the national and international societies, we can cooperatively find solutions to the major problems that confront us. In our nation we need to prepare all children to become confident, independent, participating and contributing members. We cannot afford the cost of failure. (p. 1)

As early as 1895, psychologists including Hall, Gessell, and Terman discovered that children from 10 to 15 undergo different physical and psychological changes that required different educational opportunities than were provided in traditional elementary and secondary schools (Hall, 1904). In the 1960s, William Alexander, known as the father of the middle school, advocated that junior high schools make changes in order to meet the unique needs of young adolescents and introduced the term *middle school.*

George and Alexander (1981) report that the cognitive and intellectual skills that make their appearance in the lives of many middle schoolers not only influence the manner in which they are able to deal with academically oriented abstractions and orientations; these same skills also provide young adolescents with new abilities to use in examining their sense of self with their families, friends, and teachers. Middle school students become increasingly aware of themselves and of relationships with others. Indeed, these human beings may be more aware of others during this period than during any other time of life. Not only are "Who am I?" and "Am I normal?" persistent as questions, but also "Who do you think I am?" dominates much reflection and many relations (pp. 6-9).

More recent research also notes the unique nature of early adolescence. "The emerging adolescent is caught in turbulence, a fascinated but perplexed observer of the biological, psychological, and social changes swirling all around" (Jackson & Davis, 2000, p. 6). Middle level students are acutely aware of the smallest differences between their peers and themselves; therefore differences in lifestyles, gender, race, culture, socioeconomic status, and ethnicity, to name a few, would seem to be antecedents to diverse and distinct complications for these young adolescents. "Young people undergo more rapid and profound personal changes between the ages of 10 and 15 than at any other time in their lives" (NMSA, 2003, p. 3).

"The big lie," an idea conceptualized by Charletta Phillips, a teacher and clinical psychologist from Greensboro, North Carolina, is that "virtually all young people are told that they are inadequate because they are different...it is during this time that middle level students compare themselves to others in almost every dimension of their development" (Van Hoose & Strahan, 1988, p. 21).

I. Who Are Middle Level Students?

The old and oft used cliché, "It is the best of times—it is the worst of times" defines the lives of young adolescents. *Turning Points 2000: Educating Adolescents in the 21st Century* (Jackson & Davis, 2000) reports that young adolescents ages 10-15 face a period when their lives are surrounded by confusion, disorder, turmoil, chaos, and steady change. Middle level students are acutely aware of the smallest differences between their peers and themselves. Have you ever noticed that every time middle level students walk down the hall they constantly jump to touch the top of the doors or ceilings? As Jim Garvin (1988) tells it, "It [is] important for them to see if they can touch something today they couldn't reach yesterday. More than anything else, young adolescents need to develop a view of themselves as valuable, able, and responsible people" (p. 26).

Peter Scales (1991) contends that young people move through early adolescence establishing group identity that serves as a cocoon and that young adolescents, like the "terrible twos" of infancy, also have "terrible toos...too much, too little, too slow, too fast" (p. 9). Young adolescents want too much, believe they have too little, and think their world is moving too slowly, while they are intent on moving too fast—not only through their developmental stages, but in maturing from a happy-go-lucky, wanting-to-please young child to a serious, many times isolated or isolating young person. One day that young person may be absolutely sure of everything and the next day not sure of anything. Young adolescents find themselves in situations where they are neither treated as children nor as adults. They find themselves wanting to identify as individuals yet routinely conform to dress, attitude, and activities of their peer groups. In conjunction with this newfound responsibility comes the ability to begin to reason about future life choices, develop respect for other human beings, and reflect on one's own thoughts and actions.

Increasingly, young adolescents have to deal with less support from traditional sources. Many times a single parent has more than one job just to make ends meet; "latchkey kids," with no adult at home after school, are more and more common. Because of the transient nature of families today, there are fewer opportunities that extended family members are available for young adolescents. Couple this with the constant peer pressure young adolescents experience, and it is easy to see the choices this new stage of life has thrust upon them.

Young adolescents need frequent success and recognition of their accomplishments to foster strong self-concept and self-esteem; at the same time they need help in learning to deal with the stress of added responsibility. Those who work with young adolescents must understand their unique developmental characteristics and how these traits affect their lives.

When reflecting on these characteristics, we need to understand the importance of diversity when discussing young adolescents. Just as tadpoles change to frogs and then to beautiful people, so too do young adolescents change from young children, to young adolescents, to beautiful people. *But,* they are diverse, each with his or her own kind of beauty.

How are young adolescents diverse?

What is diversity? What does it mean to be diverse? Does it refer to race? gender? culture? sexual orientation? opportunity? religious issues? values? or all of these? Diversity can be described as assorted, different, many, miscellaneous, several, unlike, various.

National Middle School Association (n.d.) defines diversity as

Diversity is the understanding that we are all different, and each person brings a unique and important perspective to life. Diversity is a positive force which is a symbol of strength and encompasses all those differences that make each of us unique. (www.nmsa.org)

Characteristics of Young Adolescents

- They are bright and curious.
- They are sensitive and aware of how they are perceived.
- They struggle with issues around ethnicity, race, and gender.
- They respond to support and exhortations to improve.
- Many assume tremendous responsibilities in their families and church communities, causing them to be more adult-like than many adults expect.
- They have high aspirations and want well-paying jobs; they do not know the instrumental steps to reach their goals.
- They are loyal, care about what significant others think of them, and do not want to disappoint these people.
- They respond to discipline, structure, and consistency.
- They respond to caring, firm, friendly adults they trust and respect and by whom they feel cared for and respected.
- They work when what they are doing has meaning in their daily lives and will help them achieve a goal or a dream.
- They learn and achieve when taught as if this is expected.
- Their parents and families are concerned and will use suggestions and respond to coaching from teachers.
- Their parents and extended families are proud when they do well and will support their efforts and achievements.

(King, Hollins, & Hayman, 1997, p. 209)

In this book we will discuss a variety of different issues and how they affect young adolescents during a time of great growth. While young adolescents may be racially and culturally diverse, they are also diverse in many other ways.

Why is it important to address diversity and how does it relate to middle school?

Gloria Ladson-Billings (1994) contends that "how teachers think about education and students makes a pronounced difference in student performance and achievement" (pp. 18-26). One of the characteristics of young adolescents is their acute awareness of themselves and anyone who is the least bit different. So, if a classroom has more than one culture, more than one gender, more than one race, more than one socioeconomic group, this could definitely affect students' learning, their social and emotional adjustment, and even how they feel about themselves.

Young adolescents who are in schools or classes comprised of only one cultural group need to learn about other cultures and ethnicities to prepare them for the world outside their own. As difficult as it is to imagine in 2004, there are young people who have never seen anyone who looks different or who thinks differently, until they go away to college or enter the military. Isn't this all the more reason for awareness of many types of diversity to be taught?

When students with physical or intellectual disabilities are mainstreamed in regular classes, both those with and without disabilities learn from each other. Students learn to be more caring, understanding, and aware of individuals and how they can be different; they also learn about their own strengths and weaknesses and how to work and learn together.

But cultures and physical and intellectual abilities and disabilities are not the only qualities that make people diverse. Family makeup—one parent or two, parents who work outside the home, adoption, expectations of the family for the young adolescent, and opportunities available to the student—all are diverse situations. Sexual orientation, learning styles and abilities, and even geographical location and accent may also be included.

One way to help young adolescents learn to accept differences of all kinds—physical, emotional, intellectual, and social—is to make them aware of books and films that help them understand their own and other cultures. At the same time, they must be careful not to reinforce misconceptions and stereotypes.

While readers may be shocked and upset by Mildred D. Taylor's (1990) portrayal of racism in the South before the Civil Rights Movement or the cruelty experienced by children who participated in the movement, as documented in Yvette Moore's

(1991) young adult novel *Freedom Songs,* or the real life memories of Sheyann Webb and Rachel West Nelson's (1980), *Selma, Lord, Selma,* these books offer different messages to white and African American children. Middle school classes can benefit from a discussion of how books and films may affect different audiences differently.

"The role of culture and how it changes under changing conditions cannot be ignored" (Miller-Lachman & Taylor, 1995, p. 317). Classrooms change daily, therefore the curriculum and the method of presenting the curriculum must also change. No longer are the majority of classrooms filled with students who all live in the same neighborhood, go to the same church, and eat the same foods. Students whose second language is English, who wear different clothes, and have different traditions are moving into previously all white neighborhoods at a rapid pace. School curricula must be adapted to reflect this change.

II. Stereotyping, Race, and Ethnicity

Recently a newscaster, reporting on a fight at a middle school, stated, "a football player and an Asian were in a fight at school today." The image of a large, "brawn and no brains" young man fighting with a small-boned young man wearing glasses and carrying a calculator is a picture that leaps to mind. This is only one of the rampant forms of stereotyping that students live with in their daily lives, and the media does little to combat it.

In many areas of the United States minorities have become the majority. This is already true in areas like Dodge City, Kansas, and Ft. Morgan, Colorado. The Hispanic population in Ft. Morgan is quickly becoming the majority rather than the minority. Soon, racial, and ethnic diversity will be the norm instead of the exception in the majority of middle level classrooms across the United States and around the world.

> The early results from the 2000 Census indicate that our diversity has already increased dramatically, even within minority communities. The Latino population now equals that of African Americans; the Asian American and Pacific Islander population is on a rapid ascent; and nearly seven million Americans checked more than one racial box in the census that first allowed this possibility."
> (Ninety-eighth American Assembly, 2002, p. 5)

According to a report from *State Profiles of Public Elementary and Secondary Education—1996-97,* demographics for five different states including New York, Pennsylvania, Georgia, Texas, and Virginia, report the minority population is quickly becoming the majority, Unfortunately, the percentage of minority teachers is not rising at the same level as the students—

from 9.2% in 1976 to only 9.3% in 1996 (p. 81). More and more we are becoming a diverse society. Teachers must be prepared to address their own biases and prejudices to work successfully with students of different races and ethnicities.

"Stereotyping," according to Miller-Lachmann & Taylor (1995), "consists of the assignment of a set of characteristics to everyone in a given racial or ethnic group. Stereotypes not only exaggerate cultural differences, they assume all members of the group share those differences, regardless of individual personality, family background, socioeconomic status, and membership in a sub-group" (p. 304). Asians, African Americans, Native Americans, and indeed all students, must be treated as individuals, not as stereotypes of their cultures. For example, middle level teachers must not expect all Asian students to be small, dark, extremely intelligent young people who excel in mathematics and computer science. Not all African American students will participate in athletic or musical events based simply on stereotypes regarding their race or ethnicity.

It is very easy to find stories or novels that stereotype around gender issues—the cute little curly haired, blonde, blue-eyed girl with the pink dress playing grownup as she sets the table, sweeps the floor, and rocks her baby doll. As she gets a little older she is seen studying to be a teacher, a nurse, or a secretary. While these are important careers, she could just as well be a doctor, engineer, or truck driver.

Until recently, textbook publishers often illustrated their books with pictures that suggested stereotyped roles for young women and men. Passive, caring, and "following orders" types of roles were filled by females, while aggressive, physical, and "giving orders" types of roles were filled by males. Given the fact that many children of color are from low income families and may have less access to other books at home, the shortcomings of basal readers become even more significant (Miller-Lachmann & Taylor, 1995, p. 285). Middle level teachers must be very watchful of the texts and tradebooks used in the classroom to ensure that stereotyping by gender, role, race, or ethnic group is not present.

Strategies for Teachers

Analyze children's books for sexism, racism, and stereotyping. The following ideas are suggested by the Council on Interracial Books for Children:

- Check for illustrations that are stereotypical or examples of tokenism. Is there a male figure depicted going to work carrying a briefcase, while a female figure stays at home with the children?

- Check the story line for standards of success: Does it depict "white" behavior, or resolutions being made only by them? Check the role of women. What is the role of minorities in the business world or in athletics? Are African Americans depicted only as athletes and musicians?

- Look at lifestyles for inaccuracies, inappropriate or oversimplified depictions of any one culture. Are Asians all depicted as small in stature, with dark complexions, and proficient in math?

- Consider who has the power, exhibits leadership, and solves problems in relationships between characters in the story. Is the leader always depicted as a white male, and the person with the problem either female or a minority?

- Whose interests are being served by the heroes? Are minority children only portrayed in universal settings or are they actually in their own cultural communities?

- What are the effects on self-image of the middle level student? Do students see persons from their cultures portrayed as heroes or heroines?

- Check the author's or illustrator's qualifications. Does this person have expertise in the subject for which he or she is reporting? Do textbook authors depict their own culture as superior?

- Check for offensive overtones in descriptions and conversations. Are clichés such as "Jew them down on the price," "Indian giver," or "Chinese fire drill" used in conversations or descriptions?

- Check the copyright date. More recently published books are often less racially or sexually offensive.

- Peruse the local newspaper to find stereotypes in writing and in advertising.

- Create an assignment where students watch a television show and identify stereotypes.

Source: www.birchlane.davis.ca.us/library/10quick.htm

III. Physical Diversity

With regard to physical characteristics, diversity is easy to see every time one walks down a middle school hallway, looks across the athletic field, or watches students rushing to the bus at the end of the school day.

Young adolescent males range from short and stout, to tall, skinny, and clumsy, from boys to young men whose muscles are fully developed. Young adolescent females also range from the small girl who carries a teddy bear and is still a child, to the young woman who is fully developed with breasts, hips, a waist, and acne, and who wonders what to do with and how to take care of all these new "attachments." Of course there are many students who don't fit either description and wonder if they ever will. Van Hoose, Strahan, and L'Esperance (2001) remind us that young adolescents will gain an average of 10 to 20 inches in height and 40 to 50 pounds in weight between ages 10 to 15. As adults we view this as a natural phenomenon, but young adolescents often worry that something may be wrong with them because of these significant physical changes. Each certainly affects how they feel about themselves.

> If they are bigger or smaller, shorter or taller than what
> they perceive to be the norm, young adolescents tend to
> think that there is something wrong with them. If they
> deviate from the norm, then they think that they are
> abnormal. Middle grades students spend a lot of time
> worrying about their physical differences—at home, and
> at school during classes. (p. 10)

Because the extremities—hands, feet, ears—grow more quickly than other parts of the body, young adolescents are often seen, and in reality feel as clumsy, with shoes the size of "gunboats" and hands that knock over everything. "It is not surprising that our students feel like 'Bozo the Clown' and think that their bodies have betrayed them" (p. 11).

Here is an example of what not to do when dealing with middle level students: A principal addressed the student body at the beginning of the school year, stressing the differences among students. Unexpectedly he called two young ladies to the stage, one quite fully developed and one who was still "waiting." Standing them back to back and locking their arms together, he declared this an example of the differences between peers! To even begin to acknowledge the multitude of feelings in the minds of those two young women is unthinkable! Embarrassed? Confused? Distressed? Mortified? Downright angry? Any or all of these feelings might have been a part of that terrible moment, and deservedly so. Whatever would possess an administrator to conduct this display of arrogance? Not thinking? Not an excuse. An episode of this nature should never happen in any school.

It is very important for middle level teachers to remember these physical differences when planning classroom activities. It is important during gym class, for example, when captains choose teams from their classmates. This situation leaves the non-athletic, over- or underweight student waiting to be the last one chosen while his or her self-esteem and self-concept take a nose dive. It is also important to remember when deciding whether to use standard desks and chairs in the classroom, where that fully developed young man mentioned earlier is picking up the desk with his knees, bouncing it around, trying to find a way to get comfortable while staying focused on learning. Middle level students would much rather be involved in hands-on, active learning than simply sitting in a desk that is too small in the first place. Is it any wonder that students find the slightest excuse to bound out of their seats to sharpen a pencil—regardless if it is in the middle of anything important?

When asked how he handled diversity in his classroom, a teacher responded, "We don't have any diversity in my classroom. We're all alike." Perhaps they are all of the same socioeconomic status, perhaps they are all males or all females, but there is no way there is no diversity in his classroom. Such attitudes lead to misunderstood and misinformed young adolescents.

Gender bias

Several teachers were videotaped to help them become more aware of how they treat boys and girls differently. The results were surprising. First of all, the teachers used completely different terminology when speaking with boys, giving more extensive verbal feedback; and, when occasions arose, boys were given leadership roles, while the girls became followers. In one science classroom, an assignment was to complete several short experiments in groups of three or four students. One such group consisted of one young man and two young women. In each experiment the young man did the actual microscope work and the two young women took notes and cleaned up the project when they were finished. It's time for a change!

Sadkar and Sadkar (1994) contend that "if a lifetime of socialization makes it difficult to spot gender bias even when you're looking for it, how much harder it is to avoid the traps when you are the one doing the teaching" (p. 4). How many times do teachers address the class with, "Okay guys, let's get to work," when in actuality they are addressing both guys and gals. Yet, they would never address this same class with "Okay gals, let's get to work." The sad part in this, however, is that seldom in such classes do young women feel there is anything wrong with being addressed as a guy. If teachers feel they must use some particular title in addressing the class, they should use "students," or, if that does not seem to fit, why use any title? Entering a classroom and stating, "Please turn to page five in your textbook," is certainly more acceptable than stating, "Okay guys, please turn to page five in your textbook." Stop and think about it. Since this is such a universal method of addressing groups of students as well as adults, it is important to be aware of what we are saying.

We must make classrooms places where both boys and girls are equal. Because of the attention given to the inequality of girls and the notion that boys do not need the consideration that girls need, girls have become the victims and boys the tyrants. One young man stated that there is now one true minority—boys. He said, "No one does anything special for us," yet boys are always being blamed for what is wrong with girls—their education, their athletics, their self-esteem. If we ensure that our classrooms foster gender equity, we can then help adolescent boys and girls develop their identities in areas free from stereotypes and open to new ideas and challenges. We must make this happen.

Strategies for Teachers

- Ask a colleague to observe your classroom, looking for ways that boys and girls are and are not treated equally.

- Do you call on boys or girls more often?

- Do you respond to boys and girls in the same way?

- Do you consistently respond to individuals of one gender or the other who shout out answers?

- Do you spend more time assisting boys or girls?

Exceptionalities

Students with physical, intellectual, visual, or auditory disabilities present a type of diversity in the middle level classroom that many teachers fail to acknowledge as a diversity. When teachers state, "We have no diversity in our classroom; we are all alike," the question should be raised as to whether all students have the same physical, intellectual, visual, and auditory capabilities. Is one student allowed to sit nearer the front to accommodate poor eyesight or poor hearing? Is tracking commonplace, thereby placing some students in classes that offer them more opportunities and others fewer opportunities?

What about inclusion? If a school district upholds inclusion, thereby mainstreaming young people with learning disabilities, mental retardation, cerebral palsy, autism, and other exceptionalities into the regular classroom, there is indeed diversity in the classroom. As mentioned earlier, just looking into any classroom will show students with absolutely no physical or athletic prowess as well as those with an ample supply. These, too, are types of diversity that must be addressed if all students are to have equal opportunities to learn and be successful.

Strategies for Teachers

- Remember individual differences. Is there an opportunity for slower or less popular students to shine in the classroom? Is it possible to find a strength in a student who is never a leader that would allow him or her to be a leader for a day?

- Investigate a downtown area for handicapped access for those who are blind, use wheelchairs, or are hearing impaired. For example, how easy is it to enter the post office or bank when on crutches or in a wheelchair? Does the automatic door open outward, thereby making it impossible for a person in a wheelchair to enter? Do crossing lights flash for those hard of hearing, or ring for those who have difficulty seeing?

- Check the employment ads to determine if companies or organizations state they have Equal Employment Opportunity (EEO). Using the Newspaper in Education program, check the want ads. Do they have the letters EEO in them? Which ones do or do not?

- Teaching *all* students how to set goals should be a priority in every classroom, especially for those students who assume they will never reach their goals. Starting out with small, reachable goals will allow for success that may help students set bigger and more enduring goals.

IV. Intellectual Diversity

During the middle level years "students first develop powers of abstract reasoning...[they] think about thinking, and that often confuses them" (Van Hoose, Strahan, & L'Esperance, 2001, p. 27). This chapter focuses not only on the intellectual development of young adolescents, but also on how intellect is affected by their cultural and geographical differences, their learning abilities and styles, the need for diversity among their teachers and administrators, as well as school climate and family expectations.

A white 13-year-old moved from Maine to southwest Virginia. A white 13-year-old moved from the mountains of Tennessee to New York City. An African American student moved from Los Angeles to southwest Colorado. A Chinese student entered a new school when his parents were hired at a local college. An Hispanic student entered a new school in mid-semester. Do these students add to the diversity in the classrooms they enter? Absolutely!

Cultural differences, speaking accents, and dealing with connotations of words and phrases are different for students in new geographical areas and different cultural situations. To add to these scenarios, imagine the turmoil in the minds of young adolescents who do not speak English. The African American student moving to southwest Colorado might have to deal with issues of color as well as the meanings of words and phrases typically used in one area and not in another. Acknowledging the importance of fitting in, middle level students will go "to the ends of the earth" before letting a group of their peers know they don't know what is happening in the daily course of events. For example, young adolescents from Maine would ask for a soda. In

Colorado, they would ask for a "pop." As minor as it might sound to an adult, to a middle level student knowing the terminology is extremely important—another way to fit in.

Recently a student teacher prepared his first lesson plan on syllabication, and his teacher reminded him to remember his geographical location. Southwestern Virginians often use more syllables in their words than, for example, northern New Englanders who naturally shorten words in their vocabulary. As a teacher from Maine who moved to Colorado and then to a Virginia university, I always model my instructions by beginning my teacher preparation classes with, "If you don't understand something I say, be sure to ask me, because I will have to ask you, I'm sure." Adults are more apt to recognize they do not understand and then ask questions. Middle level students are not as apt to speak up.

"Sit up straight and look at me when I'm talking to you!" How many times have you heard a teacher say that to a restless middle level student whose main interest is anywhere except in that classroom at that particular time? What of the child whose culture discourages looking someone in the eye, especially one's elders? What of the child whose religion forbids looking at members of the opposite sex? All these factors must be taken into account when working with middle level students.

Likewise, this issue is critical when discussing, administering, and assessing standardized tests. Inner city middle schoolers, for example, have a much different background from a middle schooler from the Midwest or deep South. These conditions should be taken into consideration whenever we examine test results for students.

Learning abilities and styles

Howard Gardner (1983) has done a great deal of work with multiple intelligences that describes eight different ways students learn. Gardner's categories include

Verbal-Linguistic	Special abilities in reading, writing, listening, communicating with words
Mathematical-Logical	Reasoning, logic, problem solving, patterns

Spatial	Visualizing, drawing, maps, imagining things
Bodily-Kinesthetic	Using body language and movement to express thoughts and ideas
Musical	Using rhythm and music to communicate
Interpersonal	Ability to understand other people
Intrapersonal	Understanding oneself
Naturalistic	Understanding and identifying nature

(Armstrong, 1994, pp. 2-3)

One way for middle level teachers to help all students be successful is by matching Gardner's learning styles to students' learning styles. Learning styles may help the unique learning needs of special needs students who may be gifted but have learning disorders, making it difficult for them to work to their potential, or gifted students who often feel isolated.

What of the teacher who frequently uses cooperative learning techniques but discovers a particular student prefers to work in isolation? Does the teacher insist the student work in a group because it more readily fits *her* teaching style, or does she allow the student to work individually as long as the student is learning and completing the work? Will the student be successful working in a group? Will the group be successful if all members do not participate? What of the highly intelligent student whose mother insists she not work in cooperative learning groups with "those dummies?" Does the teacher take the time to explain to the parent that not only will the slow learners learn more by being in cooperative learning groups, but her daughter will also learn by hearing different points of view?

It is a difficult situation, especially in middle level schools where students struggle to find their identity, to deal with yet another label. The Carnegie Council on Adolescent Development

(1989) recommended in the original *Turning Points* that tracking
be eliminated and teachers use cooperative learning strategies.

> ....all students contribute to the group effort because
> students receive group rewards as well as individual
> grades. High achievers deepen their understanding of
> material by explaining it to lower achievers; those of
> lower achievement receive immediate tutoring from
> their peers and gain a sense of accomplishment by
> suggesting solutions to problems. (p. 50)

Another problem with tracking identified by research is that
young, less experienced teachers are often assigned the lowest
tracks; expectations for this group of students are often much
lower, thus the students live down to the teacher's expectations of
them. Because curriculum in the lower tracks may often be dull
with little connection to students' real lives, they become bored
and often discover yet another reason to tune out.

Strategies for Teachers

- Use cooperative learning groups that involve students
  from all learning abilities and styles. "Real life" is a
  community effort of people from all walks of life and all
  intelligences.

- Give students opportunities to write regularly in a journal
  to which you respond. This journal should be confidential
  so that students will be encouraged to write freely.

- Plan to do an integrated or interdisciplinary unit with
  other teachers. If students can see how disciplines relate
  both to each other and to real life, learning will be more
  meaningful to them.

- Plan exchanges with inner city schools. Students from
  rural areas and students from inner city schools have
  much to learn from each other. Teachers from each area
  might arrange an exchange to learn more about their
  respective schools, communities, and cultures.

- Plan longer student exchanges with students from different groups—band, choir, athletic teams, math teams, debate teams, drama clubs, yearbook.

- How about two seventh (or sixth or eighth) grade teachers swapping classrooms for a six- or nine-week period? Make arrangements with the principal and begin your planning.

- Participate in community workshops on cultural pride.

- Start a Student Diversity Club. The club could invite guest speakers; members could sponsor Diversity Days in their own schools and involve many students in the activities of the club.

V. Emotional Diversity

Moodiness, restlessness, and erratic, inconsistent behavior are elements of middle level students' emotional development. Even as they are supposedly rejecting their families and other adults, they are, in fact, seeking adult acceptance and searching for role models. At the same time, middle level students tend to be idealistic and begin to ask questions about the meaning of life.

Young adolescents often experience mood swings—not just on a daily basis, but almost minute by minute. When a young woman arrives in her middle level classroom with a smile on her face and in a happy mood, there is no reason to believe she will still be in that same mood by lunchtime, or even by the end of first period. Because young adolescents are immensely self-conscious, often lack self-esteem, and are so very sensitive, a single, negative remark or suggestion by a classmate can ruin an entire day.

Emotional well-being is tied directly to young adolescents' self-concept and self-esteem. If we perceive ourselves as a successful parent or teacher, our self-concept is high. If, on the other hand, situations arise where we feel we are not successful in these self-appointed roles, our self-concept could be nearer the bottom of the scale. If we apply this same definition to young adolescents in middle school, and if we consider the variety of roles to which they assign themselves every day, it is little wonder their self-concepts are not always at a high point. Every day young adolescents find it impossible to be the best student, the prettiest girl, the best athlete, the best daughter, and the wisest club leader, all at once. Given these impossible tasks, is it any wonder why young adolescents are on emotional roller coasters? Many feel that if they fail to be the best in anything they do, then they have failed in everything they do.

Middle level students today, because of conditions not of their own making, find themselves dealing with stress not even considered by their age group a few years ago. The percentage of families where both parents work has increased tenfold. The number of one-parent families, whether single mother or single father, continues to rise, many times adding even more stress to parents as well as to children. Recent research also documents the number of children being raised by their grandparents, with no parent present, as another phenomenon to be considered when discussing young adolescents' emotional well-being. The security of a family is no longer guaranteed. Young adolescents who decide that separation and divorce are their fault and vow to bring their parents back together feel even more disappointment, more despair, and more stress when their attempts fail.

> A natural tension exists between what a youngster perceives others as believing and his or her own personal, private hunches. Alternative explanations, multiple solutions to a problem, assertions that are contrary to fact—all these deliberations become increasingly accessible to young adolescents pondering their existence and taking personal belief positions about matters that have ethical content. From all of this thought, personal principles may emerge, even if they are articulated only to settle a momentary issue.
>
> (Stevenson, 1998, p. 86)

Beane and Lipka (1986) conducted several interviews with young adolescents over seven years, asking young adolescents to "tell me about yourself." They found the majority of survey participants concentrated on describing themselves in terms of "things I have" and "things I do not have." Is it any wonder then, that the young adolescent who describes himself or herself by "things I do not have" and "things I cannot do" will have a low self-concept and low self esteem?

It becomes more and more evident that if teachers provide avenues for young adolescents to be successful in school, it will create a successful platform on which to build future successes.

Religious issues

With increasing numbers of young adolescents from diverse cultures, religions, and ethnicities attending classes together, it is important that the majority culture not set expectations and standards to which all middle level students cannot comply. Often middle school students' emotional well-being hinges on being accepted in such areas as dress, food, and holidays. If students have different religious or ethnic beliefs concerning fashion, how boys and girls interact with each other, or with certain holidays, it is important these differences are recognized and those who believe in them are not made to feel less important or embarrassed. If school lunches are served without consideration of certain religious holidays and beliefs, it is equally important to be sure alternative choices are available. Some choices we make inadvertently cause students to have low self-concept or self-esteem, or feel left out. When students are asked, "What are some of the traditions you observe at Christmas?" are we asking only the Christians in the class to answer? What of the Jewish students? The Asian-American students? The Muslim or Seventh Day Adventist students? All students need to be included when planning celebrations of any nature.

At the beginning of the school year, I had all my students in the advisory program tell me their birthdays. Students then had the option of what type of dessert they would like to share with the group—ice cream, cake, pie, cookies, Baked Alaska, fudge, or whatever else they might choose. On the appointed day, I would bring in the birthday dessert, and the whole group would celebrate. However, one year I was brought up short—one of my new students belonged to a religion that did not celebrate birthdays, Christmas, or any other holiday. As a rural Mainer, this was my first experience with this religious belief. It certainly made me stop and think about how this young man could be included and still not compromise his family's religious beliefs. How could I sustain his emotional well-being and still have him accepted by his peers?

Halloween is another celebration that causes some groups to question activities that occur in our schools. It is extremely important to be very careful not to offend those families who are concerned about witchcraft and Satanism. As innocent as the customs of Halloween may seem, the idea of going door-to-door asking for handouts may be very insulting and offensive to some people. Many schools have now disallowed Halloween celebrations in schools, turning instead to UNICEF collections, community family events, and in some cases, no celebrations at all.

As the Easter season arrives, what a wonderful opportunity to also discuss Passover and perhaps invite persons of various faiths to talk to the class. How much more acceptance and recognition would students feel in this instance? Do we have children of other faiths who have similar holidays? Do some research and celebrate that day or season as well.

Values

Early adolescence is also a time when 10- to 15-year-olds are searching for the values they will live by as they grow into adulthood. Because they are very emotional, very sensitive, and very aware of the world around them, young adolescents ask those complicated "why" questions of parents, clergy, coaches, and teachers. Answering a young adolescent's question with "because I said so" or "that's just the way it is" is not satisfactory. Because youth are in the process of moving from concrete to abstract thinking, they now have questions that may have no answers, or at least not black and white answers. With all the challenges they encounter, young adolescents deserve honest and straightforward answers from adults for questions they ask.

Middle school students want to save the world. They are convinced they can find a way no one else has thought of to bring about change; and in some cases, they are successful. Environmental issues, such as saving the rainforest and animal rights are perfect for middle level students. They are extremely idealistic and passionately sure they can save the world, or at least make it a better place to be. Topics of this nature allow them opportunities to see connections between what they are learning and the world they live in—an important factor when choosing curriculum for middle level students. We need to capitalize on their wide-ranging interests.

Strategies for Teachers

- Investigate religious differences in your community. Have your students conduct a demographic survey to discover how many different religious groups there are. Then do research on the individual groups to become aware of their histories.

- Invite local religious leaders to your classroom to discuss traditions, customs, and beliefs of their religions.

- Research cultural celebrations. Cooperative learning groups could each be assigned to research various celebrations such as Kwanzaa or Cinco de Mayo. Be sure to research *all* cultures and religions in your community.

- Use community speakers in cultural celebrations. Are there community leaders who practice specific traditional celebrations in their homes who would be willing to talk to your students?

- Develop lesson plans that involve students in making a change where they can see concrete results. For example, a school group is involved in Habitat for Humanity and includes middle grades students as workers. Beans and Rice is a volunteer program where students of all ages from the local university to high school and middle grades students work at least three hours a week to help minority children with homework and social skills.

VI. Social Diversity

In his book *Learning To Kiss A Frog,* Garvin (1988) explains to parents that "...between the ages of 11 to 15, one of the strongest determinants of human behavior is peer influence" (p. 19). Young adolescents constantly ask "Who am I" Who do you think I am? Where do I fit in this society? Where can I make a difference?"

In response to the turbulent changes they experience in their physical and intellectual development, young adolescents experience dramatic changes in self-concept. More than anything else, young adolescents need to develop views of themselves as valuable, able, and responsible people (Purkey & Strahan, 1986, p. 33).

Van Hoose, Strahan, and L'Esperance (2001) point out,

> Young adolescents don't define themelves in a vacuum. Rather, they define their identity based, to a large extent, on how "significant" others convey their perceptions of them. Parents/caretakers, friends, teachers, and other family members play key roles in their personal development....Identity acts as "an unfolding bridge" linking individual and society, childhood, and adulthood. (p. 45, 47)

Young adolescents want to be identified as individuals yet conform to dress, attitude, and activities of their peer groups. The desire to interact comfortably with their peers yet still be individuals with their own autonomy is extremely critical in the lives of these young adolescents. Their loyalty is shifting from family to peers; and finding approval and encouragement from their peers is of utmost importance. Even while they are feeling that adults do not believe or understand them, they still seek out adult role models, often using parental supervision as an excuse when they are unsure of situations in which they find themselves. For example, when asked to attend a certain party or go out with a group of peers, many times young adolescents will say, "My parents won't let me," secretly happy they don't have to do something they were really not sure they wanted to do, yet they have someone besides themselves to blame. They want to feel responsible for making their own decisions, but it is still important to be able to depend on support from parents.

Changing social development

Suddenly they are dating and going out with their friends; these outdated phrases mean "hanging out with." It is sometimes difficult to figure out, however, just when they are going out, as dating is often restricted to school events, talking on the phone, or going to classes and lunch together. Of course, they can be "going out with" Jimmy or Joanne in the morning and all of a sudden they are "going out with" Bill or Susan by afternoon. It is no laughing matter, believe me! Seventh-grade girls can produce some of the most profuse tears in an extremely short period of time. Another modern change is the great number of girls calling boys for dates rather than boys calling girls. Girls have become, in many instances, the dominant factor in relationships, whether adolescent or young adult.

Middle level students still depend on their families for their values. While they are firmly loyal to their peers, and in an attempt to be different, they actually become just like everyone else, which was the goal in the first place. As their friendships go through normal ups and downs, the adults in their lives must not interfere but help them to understand that one disagreement doesn't have to ruin a relationship.

In times of unhappiness when something has happened that affects any one of a group of young people, it is not uncommon to find all of them in a sad state of tears and distress. A teacher once asked a young girl why she was crying and her reply was, "Because Sandy is." If one is doing something, it is not uncommon for an entire group to be involved in doing the same thing, just because.

No matter how many times young adolescents tell us they want to be different and "not like everyone else," when we observe a classroom or a cafeteria in a middle school, we wonder "where is the difference she was talking about?" They are all so different that they look exactly the same. The quickest way to be sure young adolescents wear the latest fad, however, is for adults to tell them we don't like it. They will run to the nearest mall to buy whatever we said didn't look good—proof positive that if parents and teachers don't approve, their peers certainly will.

As young adolescents develop mental and physical maturity, many times their social skills are still in the beginning stages. The next time you see that young man with whom you previously discussed the philosophical reasoning behind Einstein's theory, he may be acting more like a three-year-old than a 13-year-old. You wonder, "is that the same young man?" Yes, it is. It will take time for all of his attributes—physical, intellectual, emotional, and social—to catch up and develop before he becomes a mature young adult.

According to National Middle School Association (2003), one of the most critical characteristics of young adolescents in their social development is their desire for recognition for their efforts and achievements. However, not all young adolescents want or will accept the same type of recognition. Howard Johnston often says there is always something we can "catch a kid doing right" in order to acknowledge these young people, even if it is passing in homework for the first time that semester. Praising Johnny for his first good math paper or Sandy for her science project explaining the uses of electricity in space are equally as important. James, on the other hand, may not want any public acknowledgment at all. Young adolescents are extremely diverse in their accomplishments as well as in their need to be acknowledged. It is up to teachers to know their students and how they may best be helped. As stated earlier, young adolescents need to feel valuable if their existence is to have meaning. For Johnny and Sandy, sometimes even a pat on the back or a "well done" is all that is necessary to bring a smile to the face or a twinkle to the eye, whereas James may best be served by a simple nod of the head.

Finding an identity

Perhaps one of the most difficult factors creating social diversity that some young adolescents experience is their sexual orientation. Some believe that as many as ten percent of the population is gay, lesbian, or bisexual. Gay and lesbian young people commit suicide five times more often than their heterosexual peers. At a time when all young adolescents are trying to figure out who they are and what they will become, the added pressure from questions about their sexual orientation is even more confusing. Where and to whom do they turn to ask questions? To parents who may refuse to acknowledge their dilemma or, in a worse case scenario, kick them out of the house? To teachers who, many times, are afraid to even discuss homosexuality for fear of losing their jobs? To the guidance counselor who may, unfortunately, tell the student, "It's okay. You'll grow out of it." It is important that students know how to find the information they need when they need it. This is a fact of life and will not be solved by refusing to discuss such contentious issues.

When a young adolescent from India, Asia, or Africa enrolls in an American school, it provides a perfect oppportunity to broaden diversity in the classroom. Sometimes these students come from outstanding schools, but sometimes they are children of immigrants who, even though they were well-respected and gainfully employed in their native country, find themselves without jobs, unable to understand English, and now living in less than desirable conditions. Teachers need to place these young people in situations where they will succeed, where they will be able to learn English and do well in their school work, and where they will socialize with their peers, regardless of the fact they feel they are different. When a child from India enrolled in one class, the teacher used it as the perfect opportunity to begin a social studies unit on India—its culture, traditions, government, religion, and more. The young girl was able to contribute ideas and information no textbook could ever have supplied. This student was so excited that she felt welcomed and so proud that her new peers turned to her for information and asked her questions. It was a successful situation for all involved.

Identity and a sense of belonging are of utmost importance to 10- to 15-year-olds. If Jimmy has to go to school with jeans sporting the wrong label because that is all his family can afford, he is not only going to feel isolated but in all probability will also endure a good amount of teasing by his peers. How will Jimmy sit in class and learn all there is to learn if he is concentrating on jeans, sneakers, or the football jacket he does not have? Are these students at risk? Are these the students who will "fall through the cracks" of our educational system? By the time students reach middle school, it is fair to say they know if they don't have the same opportunities as the rest of their peers. They know there is a good chance they won't ever finish high school. One young girl told her teacher that she knew she wouldn't graduate anyway, so why not get pregnant now and be able to leave school. "At least I will have someone to love and someone who loves me." This must not be her only option.

The changing family

How many teachers can report that most of their students come from two-parent families where one parent is working and the other is at home to offer snacks, ask questions, and provide the necessary support at the end of the school day? Middle level students need this support just as much as younger children and perhaps even more. On the other hand, how many teachers report that there are several students in their classes who have only one parent living at home because there has been a death or a divorce in the family? Or perhaps there never has been a second parent in the home. What about students who live in a car or a homeless shelter?

What of the family with transracially adopted children? Does that create a social problem for these young people because they are different from the rest of their classmates and also from their immediate family members? One African American female who was interviewed when she was in her twenties, reported she was adopted by a loving and large Irish American family when she was very young. The family lived in what she called a "lily white" community. She stated that all through her middle school and high school years, she never once was invited to a school dance or a prom. She was "too black" for the white community and "too white" for the African American community. Although her adopted mother told her it would be better once she was in college, that did not happen either. It was the same predicament. Did this affect her? You bet! Does it affect her still? You bet! Could anything have been done to alleviate this situation? With a rising number of transracially adopted children, this is a question with which adoptive parents will continue to struggle—how to provide well-rounded, accepting, and successful lives for their children.

Another transracial child was adopted from an orphanage in Korea when he was seven years old. His adoptive parents reported he had all the food, clothing, and toys he needed, but no physical bonding. As he grew into his young adolescent years, he still had not achieved the social skills necessary to be successful. Only after attending an alternative school and receiving hours and hours of therapy did he begin to adjust and gain the social skills he so sorely needed. When talking with this young man, it is apparent the depth to which these experiences affected him during his middle school years. Was this young man interested in math or science? Not really. He was interested in how he could "fit in" and be like the rest of his peers. It takes a lot of caring and concern not only on the part of the parents, but also from teachers, guidance counselors, and administration to seek out these students and find a way to help them become successful young adults.

Family expectations

What one family expects of a son or daughter can be totally opposite from what another family might expect. Many times parents remember what it was like for them when they were in a middle level school, and this is not what they want for their children. If parents attended a traditional, departmentalized junior high school, and now their young adolescents come home talking about interdisciplinary units, saying they don't go to math class but do a lot of math in English class, parents are apt to be upset.

If parents of a highly intelligent child discover their young adolescent is participating in cooperative learning activities with students of all abilities working together, many parents will assume their child is being cheated. Parents believe their young adolescent should learn with students of the same ability. They disregard the fact that by working with students of other abilities, high-achieving students also learn through social interaction and opportunities to hear and work through the thought processes of many other students.

A great many families are willing to work closely with teachers for the good of their children. They are the parents who always attend parent conferences, volunteer whenever possible as chaperones, and check to be sure their sons and daughters bring home and finish their homework. Those parents are willing to get involved in their child's education; more school districts must find ways to get more parents to this level.

Strategies for Teachers

- Initiate student-led parent-teacher conferences. A middle school in Colorado had students create portfolios beginning in the sixth grade. Each spring students would invite their parents, aunts, uncles, siblings, or grandparents and present, along with one of their teachers, samples illustrating their work in the last year. By the time students finished eighth grade, there was ample evidence of their progress, learning, and readiness to enter high school.

- Open communication between parents and the school by sending frequent newsletters to parents. Newsletters should be available in languages of all students. Also establish homework hotlines, and invite parents into the school for chats over tea or during special programs.

Parent involvement

A prevailing myth of early adolescence is that 10- to 15-year-olds increasingly turn to their peers for guidance. However, the Carnegie Council (1989) reminds us "young adolescents need greater autonomy, they neither need nor desire a complete break with parents and families" (p. 67).

Parents need opportunities to make meaningful decisions on issues and problems concerning their children's education. In order to keep parents informed, teachers cannot rely on young adolescents to transmit important information. How many times have teachers insisted on a cleanout time for backpacks and found notices and reminders in May of events that happened back in October? Find ways to inform parents of what is going on in your schools. In order to offer families opportunities to support learning at home and at school, one school district in Alabama invites parents into classes, with parents learning right along with students.

Parents should never be placed in the middle between teachers and students. We plan parent and teacher conferences and complain because parents do not attend, even though the conferences are scheduled during the day when most parents work. We must find a way to be more flexible if we want parents involved with their youngsters. One middle school made sure at least two of the scheduled parent-teacher conferences were on a Thursday night and a Saturday morning because of parents' work schedules. An additional dilemma arises when parents arrive for a scheduled appointment only to be faced with a table of five to eight persons who *appear* ready to "do battle." In such a situation parents tend to either "fold" or become defensive. One parent suggested that teachers remember what it is like going into a doctor's office, not knowing what, if anything, is wrong, and then not understanding the terminology used to explain the ailment. When talking with parents, teachers must forget the jargon when discussing students and their needs.

Even as some parents are terrified of attending parent conferences, some teachers are terrified of communicating with parents. Many teachers worry that if parents are invited to participate in curriculum planning, they will somehow take over and demand a return to what and how they were taught when they were in junior high school.

By involving parents as partners in the education of middle level students, the goals for our students will be reached— successful students who are also lifelong learners.

Strategies for Teachers

- Accept parents as equals. Avoid "educationese." Explain concepts such as interdisciplinary teams, advisory, and portfolios in simple, straightforward language.

- Show appreciation for parental support and volunteerism. When you have eighth grade recognition, also recognize those parents who have supported and volunteered for school activities and field trips

- Establish a parent-teacher group. These groups, are a great help in letting the community at large know what is happening in the local middle school.

- Begin a Homework Hotline. Automated phone systems offer an easy to use and reliable way for parents and students to check on their homework every day.

- Make the school Web page accessible to parents. Some families will not have access to the Internet and will need special consideration if information is available only on school Web pages.

- Provide evening or weekend appointments for parent-teacher conferences. With more and more families having both parents working and with more single parent families, it is important to schedule evening or weekend parent-teacher appointments.

Diversity of faculty, staff, administration

The faculty, staff, and administration of urban schools, like those of every school, should reflect the racial and ethnic makeup of their student populations. When students from multiple cultural groups see diversity among teachers and other adults in the building, working side-by-side, they learn essential life lessons. Recently, while visiting an urban school, it was interesting to note that the only African American adults were cafeteria workers and custodians, but not a teacher of color in sight. Students need to see different types of people working together at different jobs so they understand that the lessons they learn in school about diversity are important in real life.

A safe haven

With these concerns in mind we strive to provide a safe haven in schools with a climate that allows personal growth, academic achievement, and intellectual development, where middle level students know they can develop close, caring, and trusting relationships with teachers, parents, peers, and their communities. Middle level students are changing at such a rapid rate, not only from year to year, but from day to day, in all areas: physical, intellectual, emotional, and social. They are experimenting with all types of venues, sexuality, drugs, and relationships. If adults do not provide the cushion young adults need, they will surely be at risk of slipping through the cracks.

In *A Tribe Apart,* Patricia Hersch (1999) completed an extensive study of eight teenagers in Reston, Virginia, over a period of three years. Her conclusions are that teens are indeed "a tribe apart." She states that "adults have pulled away, relinquishing responsibility and supervision, allowing the unhealthy behaviors of teens to flourish" (front flap). By becoming totally familiar with the teens in her study, she was able to observe in the most fundamental ways their routines and functions, as well as listen to their thoughts and ideas, their fears, and their questions. While most of us cannot spend either the time or the energy to replicate Hersch's study, we can learn as much as possible about the young people we deal with each day.

What of the middle schooler down the street? Do we brand him as trouble just because he is a middle schooler who has so much excess energy that he runs everywhere he goes? So what if he has long hair and an earring—does that mean he is "trouble?" Do we take the time to get to know him? A middle schooler once told me she wore too much makeup and dyed her hair purple just to see how others would react. Makeup and hair dye can be washed off, but if young people get a permanent label just because they experimented with clothes and style, they will indeed become more likely to "fall through the cracks." Middle schoolers can be fascinating, funny, and fantastic young people if given a chance—a chance to know that people care about them and what they are doing, a chance to safely experiment with ideas and inspirations, and a chance to search for the meanings of who they are and who we think they are.

Van Hoose, Strahan, & L'Esperance (2001) came to the conclusion that

> Young adolescents form a healthy sense of identity
> when they can address their needs for competence,
> autonomy, and social support. In spite of their apparent
> buoyancy, they are fragile, perhaps more fragile than
> at any other time in their lives. ...the most successful
> schools and the most successful teachers in the middle
> grades are those who meet young adolescents' needs for
> security, support, and success in a proactive manner.
>
> (p. 63)

Strategies for Teachers

- "Be where you don't have to be." Attend school dances, athletic contests, non-athletic events, social and academic events to let the students know you care about them and are interested in them.

- Create an after-school program for middle schoolers. Student teachers in one Virginia county work two afternoons a week with middle grade students who need extra academic and social skills help. The first half hour is devoted to academic help with homework, and the second half hour is recreational where the student teachers and the students get to know each other on a more personal level.

- Offer to tutor middle school students. Contact the local high school or a nearby university to engage tutors. Eighth graders can work with seventh and sixth graders, and seventh graders can work with sixth graders.

- Use an advisory meeting to address and discuss social issues concerning young adolescents. Use these excellent resources:

— *Treasure Chest: A Teacher Advisory Source Book* (Hoversten, Doda, & Lounsbury, 1991. Published by NMSA—available at www.nmsa.org). An entire notebook dedicated to activities to get young adolescents involved and working with each other.

— *I am Gifted, Creative, and Talented* (Hooker & Gallagher, 1984. Published by Educational Design—available at www.amazon.com). This book has several excellent activities to begin discussions on social issues.

VII. Developing a Diverse Curriculum

C urriculum is the most important component of any school; working in conjunction with organizational and school climate, the curriculum stands the biggest chance of making profound changes in student learning.

> Curriculum that meets the needs of young adolescents is based on criteria of high quality that provide direction for what young adolescents should know and be able to do and help them achieve the attitudes and behaviors needed for a full, productive, and satisfying life. (National Middle School Association, 2003, p. 24)

Banks and Banks (1997), in the excellent curriculum resource on culturally competent teaching in "transformative" and "social action" approaches to changes in classroom curriculum, suggest four levels for integrating ethnic content into the curriculum.

Level 1: Contributions Approach is characterized by adding ethnic heroes into the curriculum but limited primarily to special days, weeks, and months related to ethnic events and celebrations. Students study little or nothing about the event or celebration before or after the occasion, and the curriculum remains unchanged in terms of its basic structure, goals, and characteristics. These events and issues are considered "add-ons" to the core curriculum. The contributions approach also tends to miss important concepts and issues related to cultural groups, and often results in reinforcing stereotypes and misconceptions by stressing the strange and exotic. Banks and Banks (1997) notes, "The criteria used to select ethnic heroes for study and to judge them for success are derived from the mainstream society and not from the ethnic community" (p.233).

Activities of this type often include surface attention given to well-known cultural heroes and heroines such as Sacajawea, Booker T. Washington, Cesar Chavez, or Benjamin Bannaker. Teachers might create a unit on "Native American Heroes," or "Women Who Have Made a Difference." Cultural foods, dances, and music are added to the curriculum.

Level 2: Ethnic Additive Approach. Without changing the basic structure, purposes, and characteristics of the curriculum, cultural events and issues are added using the perspective of mainstream culture. These additions do not include views and perspectives from diverse cultural groups, nor illustrate the roles played by these groups in the history and formation of society as we know it today. Banks and Banks (1997) call this the "illusion of inclusion."

Activities at level 2 include strategies from the contributions approach mentioned earlier, adding a book or video to the curriculum with no change in perspective, including words and phrases from other cultures such as spelling lists, and having a class cooking project use recipes from different cultures (Banks & Banks, 1997). While levels 1 and 2 are relatively simple add-ons to the curriculum, some would argue that any step taken to include ethnic and multicultural materials and information is better than ignoring it completely.

Level 3: Transformative Approach. This approach differs primarily from levels one and two because the curriculum is changed to allow students to study concepts, issues, themes, and problems from different perspectives, thus extending their understanding of the roles played by various ethnic and cultural groups in American society.

Activities for level 3 include studying events such as the Civil War from the perspective of African Americans as well as northerners and southerners, or contrasting the reasons for the patterns of migration to the United States for people of Italian, Asian, Slavic, and African descent.

Level 4: Social Action Approach. This approach uses all the components of the Transformative Approach, adding more "student decision-making and social action-related activities regarding the concept or issue being studied." This approach requires a great deal of change in the curriculum to include materials and resources to precipitate desired outcomes—social responsibility and justice—from students.

The levels and activities suggested in each approach are excellent beginning points for creating a positive and accepting classroom climate and for extending the curriculum. While they may seem beneficial, these activities sometimes reinforce the notion that ethnic studies are not important enough to be part of the everyday curriculum. But it is the teacher's responsibility to push the level of integration ahead. Some classes are stuck at level one, focusing only on heroes like Martin Luther King, Jr. for Black History Month, or holidays such as Cinco de Mayo.

During one teacher's attempt to educate her students about African American history other than during February, a student asked, "Why do we have to learn about black history, we don't learn about white history!" It's definitely time for a change! One way to move from level 1 to level 4 is to ask students how they want to integrate content and on which issues they want to take action. Middle level students become intensely involved when they are working on issues from real life—issues that will involve them and their futures. But remember, change is a process. It will take time and much work to move from level 1 to level 4. The important point is to realize and determine that it is time to begin the change—now!

Analyze your curriculum

Banks and Banks (1997) suggest guidelines to check curriculum for bias:

- Does the curriculum include content that will encourage students' self-awareness, regardless of sex, race, culture or disability?

- Are the perspectives and contributions of diverse racial and cultural groups, both men and women, as well as those with disabilities, included?

- Does the curriculum include activities or units dealing with the recognition of stereotyping and prejudice when they appear in written and oral language?

- Are there activities that assist students in analyzing the mass media for ethnocentrism, sexism, or stereotyping of those with disabilities?

- Do speech and composition activities include content that helps students speak and write in a nonsexist and culturally sensitive manner?

- Is there career-oriented content that encourages the exploration of a broad range of careers, regardless of students' sex, race, culture, or disability? (pp. 243-247)

Strategies for Teachers

- Plan a multidisciplinary unit on your home town. Math activities include collecting demographics on something as simple as the number of telephones, televisions, or pets. For science activities students could test the drinking water. In social studies students might investigate the history of the town and where the original inhabitants came from; in language arts students could create an original play using all these facts from the different disciplines. Include technology, industrial arts, and home economics or life skills content as well as music and physical education activities to enhance the unit.

- Plan thematic units using questions such as these:
    — Is there prejudice in your town, school, or classroom? How can you and your students change it?
    — How diverse is your town, school, or classroom? How can you celebrate that diversity?

— What are the obvious relationships that occur between faculty and students? Between students and students? Among faculty and students and administration? Among parents, students, faculty, and administration?

• Contact friends or relatives in another state who might speak to a local teacher.

• Investigate e-mail sites where a teacher could help students select pen pals from other states or countries.

• Produce a play that compares the Civil Rights era of the 1960s with current civil rights legislation.

• Use video and films to illustrate diversity, for example
  — *The Shadow of Hate* (1995) (www.tolerance.org)
  — *A Place at the Table* (2000) (www.tolerance.org)
  — *Don't Laugh at Me* (2000) (www.dontlaugh.org)

• Use role playing: Using newspaper accounts of recent hate crimes, set up a courtroom scene where there is a jury, judge, accuser, and accused, as well as a reporter. Following courtroom procedure, try the case, and report the results.

• Use international artwork to explore the significant contributions made to today's society by several cultural groups. Have students view these and other masterpieces online or in art books.

— Russian-born Marc Chagall, *The Praying Jew, The Violinist*

— Spanish-born Salvador Dali, *The Crucifixion, The Sacrament of the Last Supper*

— Italian-born Leonardo Da Vinci, *Mona Lisa, Madonna and Child, The Last Supper*

— French-born Henri Matisse, *Beasts of the Sea, Creole Dancer*

— Holland-born Vincent Van Gogh, *The Starry Night*

- Use music and dance to explain similarities and differences of each cultural group represented in the classroom.
  — Italian-American band leader and composer, Louis Prima
  — German-Austrian composer, Ludwig van Beethoven
  — Viennese composer, Wolfgang Amadeus Mozart
  — Russian composer, Peter I. Tchaikovsky
  — English ballerina, Margot Fonteyn
  — Russian ballet dancer, Rudolph Nureyev

- Invite speakers from cultural groups in your community to speak to your classes. Ask parents representing various ethnic groups to speak to the class about traditions, foods, and beliefs.

VIII. Addressing Diversity in Middle Level Schools

Are we like the middle level teacher who, when asked about diversity in his classroom, replied, "We don't have any diversity in this school" simply because there were no apparent ethnic or racial differences? Do we recognize diversity as being more than just color or a different religion? How do we assure our middle level students that they will have a safe and caring environment for learning? How do we involve parents and the community when we consider diversity issues? All these questions and more arise when we consider how we currently address diversity.

Manning (1994) reported that "multicultural education, a relatively new concept, was not listed as an identifying term in the *Education Index* until 1978" (p. 39).

While diversity is a relatively new concept, it is also a hot topic in most schools and communities. Schools are more diverse —and in ways we would never have imagined possible—than ever before. Because we are now and will continue to become more and more mobile, picking up and moving with job transfers, or seeking new adventures with educational opportunities and retirement, we no longer stay in our hometowns generation after generation with people like us. Today young people must adjust to a different way of life. Because of the large percentage of families with two working parents, or families with only one parent who is also a working parent, no longer is there always someone at home after school to greet youngsters with, "How did your day go?" Many times there is no one to help with homework, no one to answer questions, no one to simply be there at the end of the day.

When young adolescents have questions about the new kid who just moved to town and is in their class, we need to stop and think just who this new kid is. Is he the new kid who is of a different race, a different culture, who eats unusual foods and dresses differently? or the new kid whose family lives in its car because dad lost his job and they can't afford to pay rent? or the new kid who is part of the school inclusion team and has been assigned the seat across the aisle? The answers we give are neither always in the best interest of either the new kids nor the young adolescent with the questions. Deciding that "different" is wrong because no one has a better definition will only diminish the potential learning experience of both the adolescent and the new student.

It has been said that children have to *learn* to hate, that hate is not a natural condition. If that is the case, it is critical to work with the families and communities of young adolescents, providing examples where people of all differences learn to get along with each other and accept each other as human beings. Many times parents are reluctant to come to school conferences simply because they do not understand English. Their "difference" sets them apart from the rest of the community, and they do not feel comfortable attending family nights or other parent conference meetings. One school district with a large number of Hispanic families sends notices of school activities home in both English and Spanish, assuring that the message is understood. On the night of the activity, an interpreter is available to ensure that everyone understands and participates. This positive action creates a win-win situation for all involved!

Over the past few years, more programs have been developed to help teachers and students find ways to answer some of these questions, establish a sense of family when there are so many different members, and help young adolescents learn to work with one another in a safe and caring space, because of and in spite of their differences. Many schools have established homework hotlines so students as well as parents can find out about assigned homework. This is especially helpful if a student has been home ill or absent from school for any other reason. Professional associations such as National Middle School Association and the Virginia Middle School Association publish newsletters with Web site resources to assist teachers in designing a more diverse curriculum. A Maine school district developed a program called Open Waters, Safe Harbors, in which students interviewed senior citizens in the community and made a video of the interviews for teachers to use in their classrooms. One particular interviewee, a German Jew, had escaped to the U.S. during the Holocaust. This gentleman agreed to speak to several middle school classes as part of the Holocaust Unit. Did this make more of an impact than simply reading from a textbook? Of course it did.

Students need opportunities to learn about other cultures, religions, races, and philosophies. They not only need to learn how it feels to be different, but they also need to learn that it is all right to be different. As a consequence, teachers from middle level schools are spending more and more time in professional development activities, attending meetings and workshops to find ways to help their students learn to work and cooperate with persons who are different from themselves. Universities and colleges are providing a new commitment to diversity in preparing teachers. They are also reaching out to diverse populations in order to present a more accurate representation of school districts with large multicultural populations.

Students in a Colorado middle school, for example, spent time in their school library analyzing fiction about stereotypes by studying book covers and predicting how issues of race and gender would be presented and what topics the books would cover. Another class had a "word for the day" noting anniversaries of special accomplishment, such as the first woman senator. As the culminating activity of an advisory project at a Maine middle school, students and teachers created a school-wide multicultural fair offering samples of foods, music, fashions, occupations, and much more from countries around the world. In helping students learn how to live and work with people from different cultures, one middle school established student peer mediation groups to aid other students who had problems dealing with differences.

The predicament facing educators today, however, is that we are still not doing enough to provide a safe, caring, and trusting learning environment for our students, teachers, staff, and parents. What next? How and where do we go from here? Even though we sometimes feel we are butting our heads against a brick wall, is there an answer?

How can we improve the way we address diversity in middle schools?

There are a number of ways we can address diversity in middle schools to make them better places to learn. Teachers must recognize their own prejudices and biases. We simply must eliminate phrases, thoughts, and perceptions such as these: "If she didn't eat so much she wouldn't be fat. Fat students are lazy." "He comes from the other side of town, down by the trailer park. Those kids don't do very well in school." "Remember his brother? No one in that family is very bright." "You know how those Hispanic kids are. Here today, gone tomorrow. No use in spending extra time with them."

What chance do students with such labels have to become successful? We must address these biases when we hear them. We must be willing to speak up when we hear anyone degrading another. And we must take advantage of such occurrences to teach ourselves that as members of the human race we each deserve consideration and respect.

One middle school in Colorado with Hispanic and African American students recognized that reducing conflict was vital so students could focus their energies on acquiring knowledge and prepare for a high school education. A team of teachers organized a culture study that extended across the curriculum to "emphasize what each culture has contributed to humanity." They further worked on reducing conflict by recognizing the multiethnic components in everyone's background. "It is not enough to say that all students are different. It is not enough to try and understand what makes them different. Teachers must somehow reach students from all kinds of backgrounds with varying degrees of limitations and potentials" (Reed, Bergemann, & Olson, 1988). Emphasizing, as the Colorado team did, what each culture had contributed to humanity is one way of reaching all students, regardless of their backgrounds.

The Dove Intelligence Test (1971) was developed to illustrate that standardized tests are biased. Test questions are based on phrasing, actions, and experiences of African Americans.

African Americans would most likely score well on this test, while young people from other backgrounds might not score as well. Likewise, it should be understood that young adolescents who grow up in an African American culture many times do not do as well on standardized tests used in schools today. There are many ways to say the same thing. If we are to address diversity in our classrooms, we must find different methods of evaluation to reach all of our students.

Strategies for Teachers

- Create a committee to select standardized tests for your school or district that are culturally unbiased.

- Select music that students can "dissect" and discuss. Mark Wills' song entitled, "Don't Laugh at Me" talks about geeks, girls with braces, single teenage mothers, and homeless and hungry street people. What a wonderful avenue for engaging young adolescents in a discussion concerning those less fortunate than themselves.

- Also, based on this same song, "Don't Laugh at Me," Peter Yarrow has created Operation Respect: Don't Laugh at Me (2000), a program for middle level students complete with video, teacher's guide, and CD which focuses on "root[ing] out violence...and...evolving a more compassionate classroom environment which also nurtures academic growth and achievement."

- Newspapers in Education (NIE) is an excellent program using local newspapers to learn in all content areas. There are activities using the want ads, using letters to Ann Landers or Dear Abby, geography projects using the sports pages, and various other ideas.

Connecting with service learning

Finally, service learning is a wonderful way to connect our students not only to the community, but in many cases, to those who may be less fortunate. Children in Head Start programs, children having trouble reading, adults who want to learn to read and write but are embarrassed to ask for help, the elderly couple who need their gutters cleaned—these are only a few of the projects middle level students can become involved in that help those in need. A seventh grade class in Maine helped to remove old tires from a former dump site. Not only did the students rid the area of unsightly old tires, they also eliminated a potential breeding ground for mosquitoes, an important contribution to the community.

Service learning is an excellent vehicle by which young adolescents can learn more about themselves, discover how they can become useful citizens in their communities, and learn about other members of the community who may be disadvantaged and need help. Service learning provides a connection to real life, which teaches young adolescents they can learn in different places and in different ways than just in the classroom.

Lipka, Beane, and O'Connell (1995) recognize the benefits of service learning for young adolescents as they progress through their school years and into adulthood.

- Planning and cooperation
- Awareness of community problems and needs
- Sense of self-worth through personal contributions to the community
- Sense of personal responsibility for quality of life
- Taking active roles to meet *real* needs of others
- Carrying real responsibility and making decisions affecting others
- Working collaboratively with adults
- Working as a group toward a common goal
- Having an opportunity to reflect critically on experiences

Make service learning a part of a good educational program at the middle level so that it becomes a habit that continues into adulthood.

IX. Where Do We Go From Here?

At the beginning of this book I described young adolescents—physically, intellectually, emotionally, and socially—and then explained many of the routes they travel during this challenging time in their lives. It is important to celebrate their lives, all the joys, frustrations, "falling downs and getting ups," their triumphs, and even their losses, as these experiences will help them grow and develop into successful young adults.

Diversity is an issue we are all faced with daily, whether in the community, the classroom, or the workplace. Therefore, strategies and activities have been included in this book to assist readers in dealing with this difficult task. There are questions, problems, "whys and why nots," and some answers and solutions. Can we find solutions that will be positive for all concerned? I think we can. If each individual is committed to change as he or she learns, much progress can be made. If we continue to research, to study, and to care about each other, and then actually put our ideas into action, I believe we can find ways where everyone **can** benefit. We must keep trying! We must keep educating! We must keep caring!

References

Armstrong, T. (1994). *Multiple intelligences in the classroom.* Alexandria, VA: Association for Supervision and Curriculum Development.

Bandeira de Mello, V. (2000). *State profiles of public elementary and secondary education.* Washington, DC: U.S. Department of Education, Office of Educational Research.

Banks, J., & Banks, C. (Eds.). (1997). *Multicultural education: Issues and perspectives.* Boston: Allyn & Bacon.

Beane, J., & Lipka, R. (1986). *Self-concept, self-esteem, and the curriculum.* New York: Teachers College Press.

Carnegie Council on Adolescent Development. (1989). *Turning Points: Preparing America's youth for the 21st century.* New York: Carnegie Corporation.

Cushner, K. (1999). *Human diversity in action.* Boston: McGraw Hill.

Dove, A. (1971). The "Chitling" test. In L.R. Aiken, Jr., *Psychological and educational testings.* Boston: Allyn and Bacon.

Gardner, H. (1999). *Intelligences reframed: Multiple intelligences for the 21st century.* New York: Basic Books.

Garvin, J. (1988). *Learning to kiss a frog.* Rowley, MA: New England League of Middle Schools.

George, P.S., & Alexander, W. (1981). *The exemplary middle school* (2nd ed.). Orlando, FL: Harcourt Brace College Publishers.

Hall, G.S. (1904). *Adolescence.* New York: Appleton-Century-Crofts.

Hersch, P. (1999). *A tribe apart.* New York: Ballantine Publishing Group.

Jackson A., & Davis, G. (2000). *Turning points 2000: Educating adolescents for the 21st century.* New York: Teachers College Press.

King, J.E., Hollins, E.R., & Haymann, W.C. (1997). *Preparing teachers for cultural diversity.* New York: Teachers College Press.

Ladson-Billings, G. (1994). *The dreamkeepers: Successful teachers of African American children.* San Francisco: Jossey-Bass

Lipka, R., Beane, J., & O'Connell, B. (1985). *Community service projects: Citizenship in action. Fastback #231.* Bloomington, IN: Phi Delta Kappa.

Manning, M. L. (1994). *Celebrating diversity: Multicultural education in middle level schools,* Columbus, OH: National Middle School Association.

Miller-Lachmann, L., & Taylor, L.S. (1995). *Schools for all: Educating children in a diverse society.* New York: Delmar.

Moore, Y. (1991). *Freedom songs.* New York: Puffin Books.

National Middle School Association. (1995). *This we believe: Developmentally responsive middle level schools.* Columbus, OH: Author.

National Middle School Association. (2003). *This we believe: Successful schools for young adolescents.* Westerville, OH: Author.

National Middle School Association. (n.d.). *NMSA's position paper on diversity.* Retrieved February 10, 2004, from www.nmsa.org

Ninety-eighth American Assembly. (2002). Racial Equality: *Public policies for the twenty-first century.* Retrieved March 18, 2004 from www.americanassembly.org/PDF/AA%20Race%20Report%20FINALPDF.pdf

Purkey, W., & Strahan, D. (1986). *Positive discipline: A pocketful of ideas.* Columbus, OH: National Middle School Association.

Reed, A.J., Bergemann, V.E., & Olson, M.W. (1988). *In the classroom.* Boston: McGraw Hill.

Sadkar, M., & Sadkar, D. (1994). *Failing at fairness: How America's schools cheat girls.* New York. MacMillan.

Scales, P. (1991). *Portrait of young adolescents in the 1990s: Implications for providing healthy growth and development.* Carrboro, NC: Center for Early Adolescence.

Stevenson, C. (1998). *Teaching ten to fourteen-year-olds.* New York: Longman.

Stone, L., & Church, L. (1968). *Childhood and adolescence.* New York: Random House.

Strahan, D., & Strahan, J, (1988), *Revitalizing remediation in the middle grades: An invitational approach*. Reston, VA: National Association of Secondary School Principals.

Taylor, M.D. (1990). *The road to Memphis*. New York: Dial Books.

Van Hoose, J., & Strahan, D. (1988). *Promoting harmony. Young adolescent development and school practices*. Columbus, OH: National Middle School Association.

Van Hoose, J, Strahan, D., & L'Esperance, M. (2001). *Promoting harmony: Young adolescent development and school practices*. Westerville, OH: National Middle School Association.

Webb, S., Nelson, R., & Sikora, F. (1980). *Selma, Lord, Selma: Girlhood memories of the civil-rights days*. New York: Morrow.

Wills, M. (1998). Don't laugh at me. *Wish you were here*. (CD-ROM). New York: Mercury Records.

Woolfolk, A. E. (1998). *Educational psychology* (7th ed.). Boston: Allyn & Bacon.

World Book Complete Word Power Library, Vol. 2. Chicago: World Book Encyclopedia.

Yarrow, P. (2000). *Operation respect: Don't laugh at me*. New York and Cambridge, MA: Operation Respect and Education for Social Responsibility.

Zeichner, K. M. (1993). *Educating teachers for cultural diversity*. East Lansing, MI: National Center for Research on Teacher Learning.

Annotated Bibliography of Young Adolescent Literature

INTELLECTUAL DIVERSITY

Armstrong, W. H. (1971). *Sour land.* New York: Scholastic.
Anson Stone is a white widower with three children. A black male teacher enters their lives and fills a lonely void but helps them face a tragic reality.

Avi. (1991). *Nothing but the truth.* New York: Avon Flare Book.
Philip hummed along with the tape of The Star Spangled Banner played each day in his homeroom. How could this minor incident turn into a major national scandal?

Brooks, B. (1984). *The moves make the man.* New York: Harper & Row.
A precarious friendship forms between an African American boy and an emotionally disturbed white boy.

Bunting, E. (1989). *The Wednesday surprise.* Boston: Houghton Mifflin.
Anna stays with her grandmother every Wednesday night. As a surprise to her family, Anna is teaching her grandmother to read.

Gibson, W. (1960). *The miracle worker.* New York: Bantam Books.
The story of Helen Keller and her teacher, Annie Sullivan.

Kassam, L. (1986). *Middle school blues.* New York: Avon Camelot Books.
After deciding middle school was like landing in the middle of a bad dream, Cindy decides to write a guidebook on how to get through it.

Krumgold, J. (1959). *Onion John.* New York: Scholastic.
Andy Rusch was happy to work in the family hardware store and play on the local baseball team, but his father wanted him to become an engineer.

Lasky, K. (1994). *Memoirs of a bookbat*. New York: Harcourt Brace.

    Harper's family have become "migrants of God" traveling around the country in their mobile home. Harper's choice of books and reading get her into trouble with her family and their organization.

Paulsen, G. (1993). *Nightjohn*. New York: Delacorte Press.

    Twelve-year-old Sarney's life as a female slave becomes even more dangerous when a newly arrived slave offers to teach her to read.

Philip, M. (1988). *Harriet's daughter*. Toronto: The Women's Press.

    Immigration, exile, culture, and identity all combine in this story of Margaret trying to help her friend escape from Canada and live with her grandmother in Tobago.

Radin, R. (1991). *All Joseph wanted*. New York: MacMillan.

    Eleven-year-old Joseph's mother's inability to read directions or street signs has complicated their lives greatly.

Rosen, M. (1995). *A school for Pompey Walker*. New York: Harcourt Brace Jovanovich.

    An old former slave, Pompey, relates how his white friend kept selling him into slavery to earn money to build a school.

Scott, V. (1986). *Belonging*. Washington, DC: Galludet College Press.

    The adjustments and reactions by a 15-year-old girl who has become deaf after recovering from meningitis.

Voight, C. (1982). *Homecoming*. New York: Scholastic.

    After being deserted by both her mother and father, 13-year-old Dicey searches for someone who will take her in and care for her and her three siblings.

Voight, C. (1981). *Dicey's song.* New York: Scholastic.

Dicey's story of taking care of her three younger siblings while traveling from Provincetown to Chesapeake Bay to their grandmother's house. Dicey discovers she needs a lot of love, trust, humor, and courage.

Walter, M. (1982). *Girl on the outside.* New York: Scholastic.

Two girls—one white, one African American—are caught up in the flurry of the 1957 integration of all-white Chatman High School in the small southern town of Mossville.

Williams-Garcia, R. (1992). *Fast talk on a slow track.* New York: Dutton/Lodestar.

Denzel Watson, a black honors student, spends the summer before college trying to raise money by selling candy. He learns a lesson in motivation and how to apply himself.

Arrick, F. (1992). *What you don't know can kill you.* New York: Bantam Doubleday.
Debra's "perfect" older sister discovers she is HIV positive, and her dreams of college and marriage to her wonderful boyfriend are shattered. This story tells how she and her family handle the tragedy.

Anonymous. (1998). *Go ask Alice.* New York: Aladdin.
A true story of a 15-year-old girl's descent into the world of drugs presented in the form of her diary.

Bauer, M. (1986). *Am I blue? Coming out from the silence.* New York: Harper Trophy.
Short stories about growing up gay or lesbian from authors Bruce Coville, M. E. Kerr, William Sleator, Jane Yolen, and others.

Beatty, P. (1992). *Who comes with cannons?* New York: Morrow.
The start of the Civil War changes the world of Truth, a 12-year-old Quaker girl from Indiana who is staying with relatives in North Carolina.

Beatty, P. (1981). *Lupita manana.* New York: Beech Tree Books.
Thirteen-year-old Lupita decides to cross the border into the United States as an illegal alien to help her poverty-stricken family.

Benjamin, C.L. (1984). *Nobody's baby now.* New York: Bantam Books
Olivia suddenly not only has to share her room with her ailing grandmother, she must also babysit her after school instead of spending time with her boyfriend.

Block, F.L. (1995). *Baby Be-Bop.* New York: HarperCollins.
Sixteen-year-old Dirk MacDonald gets ghostly visits from his dead father and great-grandmother, which helps him adjust to being gay.

Bunting, E. (1995). *Smoky night*. San Diego, CA: Harcourt Brace Jovanovich.

The value of getting along with others comes home hard to a young boy and his mother when the 1991 riots break out in Los Angeles.

Buss, F. L., & Cubias, D. (1991). *Journey of the sparrows*. New York: Dutton.

Illegal Salvadoran refugees struggle trying to make a living in Chicago after they have been smuggled into the U.S. in crates.

Collier, J.L., & Collier, C. (1994). *With every drop of blood*. New York: Bantam Doubleday.

A friendship develops during the Civil War between an African American Union soldier and the 14-year-old white boy who is transporting food to Richmond, Virginia.

Conley, J.L. (1993). *Crazy lady*. New York: HarperCollins.

A story of the developing relationship between an alcoholic mother and her retarded son with a young man who had previously teased them and treated them disrespectfully.

Creech, S. (1994). *Walk two moons*. New York: HarperCollins.

Thirteen-year-old Salamanca Tree Hill travels across the country with her grandparents, hoping to find her mother and reunite the family on her mother's birthday.

Crutcher, C. (1993). *Staying fat for Sarah Byrnes*. New York: Bantam Doubleday.

Two young people—one boy and one girl— are the "terminal uglies" and inseparable best friends. This book tells of the trials and tribulations of their friendship and how they survived.

Crutcher, C. (1995). *Ironman*. New York: Bantam Doubleday.

Bo Brewster is constantly getting into trouble and is sent to the Anger Management Group, where he learns to handle his anger and also falls in love.

Duffy, J. (1993). *Radical red.* New York: Charles Scribner.

Family abuse drives an Irish mother and daughter to work with Susan B.Anthony and the suffragette movement.

Ellis, S. (1994). *Out of the blue.* New York: Penguin Puffin Books.

After she discovers she has a 24-year-old half-sister, 12-year-old Megan tracks down her mother to see why she was never told about her sister.

Eyerly, J. (1977). *He's my baby now.* New York: Simon & Schuster.

With a newborn son, a young teenage father learns how to be a dad.

Gallo, D.R. (1993). *Join in: Multiethnic short stories by outstanding writers for young adults.* New York: Delacorte Press.

Several stories that reflect views of young adults of various ethnic backgrounds on friendship and prejudice.

Greene, B. (1991). *The drowning of Stephan Jones.* New York: Bantam Books.

The story of a young girl, Carla, and her struggle in dealing with her boyfriend's harassment of the homosexual owners of an antique shop. Also deals with how she and the other young people in town deal with the tragic ending of this harassment.

Greene, B. (1973). *Summer of my German soldier.* New York: Bantam Doubleday Books.

Twelve-year-old Patty Bergen is Jewish and befriends a young German prison escapee when his small hometown in Arkansas becomes the site of a camp housing German prisoners in World War II.

Greene, S. (1979). *The boy who drank too much.* New York: Laurel Leaf Books.

A young teenage boy is not dealing well with his alcoholic father and the fact his mother has died. He too begins the long, lonely road of destroying himself with alcohol.

Guy, R. (1973). *The friends.* New York: Bantam Books.
   Phyllisia, a 14-year-old from the West Indies, is overwhelmed by her new life in New York. Needing a friend, she meets up with white, 15-year-old Edith, a New York ragamuffin.

Hansen, J. (1980). *The gift giver.* New York: Clarion.
   Doris, a fifth grader, meets a special friend in her Bronx neighborhood, and they decide not to always go along with the crowd.

Heron, A., & Maran, M. (1991). *How would you feel if your Dad was gay?* Boston: Alyson Publications
   Relates the struggles of children who try to let their friends know a parent is gay.

Hesse, K. (1997). *Out of the dust.* New York: Scholastic.
   In a series of poems, 15-year-old Billie Jo relates her life in the Dustbowl years of the Depression in Oklahoma.

Hobbs. W. (1988). *Changes in latitude.* New York: Avon Flare Books.
   A family vacation in Mexico leads to a nightmare of discovery of the parents' problems, tragedy in saving endangered species of turtles, and anger and betrayal. Also deals with the young man's change from a cocky, selfish young man to one who wants to understand and be of help.

Hobbs, W. (1991). *Downriver.* New York: Bantam Books.
   Rebellious teenagers, formerly enrolled in a wilderness survival school team, "borrow" rafting equipment from their adult leader, steal his boots, and head for the Colorado River and the Grand Canyon rapids.

Hunt, I. (1976). *The lottery rose.* New York: Berkley Publishing.
   Georgie Burgess is abused by his alcoholic mother and her boyfriends. He wins a small rosebush in a grocery store lottery, giving him the impetus to survive.

Irwin, H. (1987). *Kim/Kimi*. New York: Puffin Books.

Sixteen-year-old Kim/Kimi, a Japanese-American, struggles to find her identity in an all-white Iowa community.

Jenness, A. (Ed.). *Families: A celebration of diversity, commitment, and love*. Boston: Houghton Mifflin.

Seventeen personal stories of relationships with similarities and differences between families who are stepfamilies, divorced families, families with gay parents, and foster families.

Kassam, L. (1993). *Odd one out*. New York: Fawcett Juniper Books.

Alison Gray is bright, pretty, and popular. She is asked to join the exclusive high school sorority club. When her boyfriend tries to win a bet by taking advantage of her, she decides to speak up about what really takes place at the initiations. She learns there is a price to pay.

Krisher, T. (1994). *Spite fences*. New York: Bantam Doubleday.

Changes begin happening to 13-year-old Maggie Pughin during the summer of 1960 in Georgia. Maggie experiences troubles with her mother and is drawn into the violence, hatred, and racial tension.

Lasky, K. (1981). *The night journey*. New York: Puffin Books.

Great-grandmother Nana Sashie tells the story of her life in Czarist Russia and the family's escape to the United States.

Levy, M. (1990). *Rumors and whispers*. New York: Ballantine/ Fawcett.

Sarah Alexander, a high school senior, must learn to deal with moving from Ohio to California, with the sudden disowning of her brother for reasons she cannot find out, and her favorite art teacher being fired because he has AIDS.

Lowry, L. (1993). *The giver.* New York: Dell.

At the Ceremony of Twelve, Jonas receives the memories shared by only one other member of his community. He discovers the society he lives in is not as perfect as he once thought.

Mazer, N. (1984). *Mrs. Fish, Ape, and me, the Dump Queen.* New York: Avon.

A young girl's uncle runs the town dump, which causes her to be teased every day. She finally becomes friends with Mrs. Fish, the school custodian, who helps her survive.

Meyer, C. (1993). *White lilacs.* New York: Harcourt Brace.

In 1921 in Dillon, Texas, 12-year-old Rose Lee, her family, and her neighborhood are forced to relocate when the whites in town decide to build a park where they live.

McKissack, P. (1992). *The dark thirty.* New York: Knopf.

A collection of ghost stories with African American themes, designed to be told during the Dark Thirty—the half hour before sunset—when ghosts seem all too believable.

Miklowitz, G. (1986). *The war between the classes.* New York: Dell.

Emiko, 17-year-old Japanese American, has fallen in love with white, blond Adam. Traditions and cultures are major issues in their relationship.

Mohr, N. (1989). *El Bronx remembered.* Houston, TX: Arte Publico Press.

Puerto Rican families living in the Bronx tell of their experiences of owning a pet hen named after their favorite Hollywood movie star, gypsies telling the future, and a young boy's humiliation at his graduation.

Newman, L. (1994). *Fat chance.* New York: Paper Star Book.

Judi Liebowitz wants to be the "thinnest girl in the entire eighth grade," until she becomes "friends" with Nancy Pratt who suffers secretly from binge-and-purge cycles of bulimia.

Paterson, K. (1991). *Lyddie*. New York: Penguin.

In the 1840s Lyddie's parents have died, and her siblings have been sent to live with other people. Lyddie is determined to work in the factory in Lowell, Massachusetts, to make enough money to reunite her family.

Sebestyen, O. (1968). *Words by heart*. New York: Bantam Doubleday.

Lena wants her classmates to know her for her "magic mind" rather than her black skin. After experiencing violence and death, she must learn how to forgive.

Shannon, G. (1989). *Unlived affections*. New York: Harper and Row.

At his grandmother's death, 18-year-old Willie discovers many family secrets, including the fact his father is gay.

Singer, B. (Ed.). *Growing up gay/growing up lesbian: A literary anthology*. New York: New York Press.

A collection of stories, poems, letters, and songs from a variety of backgrounds and ethnicities.

Soto, G. (1993). *Pool party*. New York: Delacorte Press.

Rudy Herrera is surprised and excited to get an invitation to a pool party from Tiffany Perez, the richest and most popular girl in school.

Soto, G. (1991). *Taking sides*. San Diego, CA: Harcourt Brace Jovanovich.

Lincoln Mendoza has moved from the barrio to the tree-lined streets of the suburbs and finds himself playing basketball against his old friends.

Speare, E. (1958). *The witch of Blackbird Pond*, Boston: Houghton Mifflin.

Kit, a young girl from the Caribbean, is orphaned and sent to New England to live with relatives. In a time of the Salem Witch Trials, she is seen as suspicious.

Voight, C. (1994). *When she hollers.* New York: Scholastic.

Tish's adoptive stepfather has been abusing her since she was a small child. Now she is determined to do something to stop it.

Voight, C. (1983) *A solitary blue.* New York: Scholastic.

Jeff's mother left him with his father. She disappeared for several years. When she suddenly invited him to come visit her, Jeff started to open up and feel again. Was that a mistake?

Wartski, M. (1980). *A boat to nowhere.* New York: Signet Books.

Mai, her little brother, and grandfather join a 14-year-old boy on a journey aboard a small boat from their village in Vietnam to safety.

Williams-Garcia, R. (1995). *Like sisters on the homefront.* New York: Dutton/Lodestar.

A pregnant teenager is sent south to live with her pastor uncle and his family. She learns the healing power of the family.

Willis, P. (1995). *Out of the storm.* New York: Avon Books.

Mandy and her mother are forced to move in with "cranky Aunt Bess" after Mandy's father died in World War II. A crisis turns Mandy's life around and helps her dream new dreams.

Wolff, V. (1993). *Make lemonade.* New York: Henry Holt and Company.

Fourteen-year-old LaVaugh babysits for a teenage mother to earn money for college.

Woodson, J. (1993). *The dear one.* New York: Dell.

Twelve-year-old Ferri is having to learn to adjust to a 15-year-old pregnant teenager who has come to live with her family.

Woodson, J. (1994). *I hadn't meant to tell you this.* New York: Dell.

Lena, a white eighth grader, is being sexually abused by her father. Marie, the only black girl in the class, becomes friends with Lena and learns the terrible truth.

Yeo, W. (1986). *Gypsy summer*. New York: Scholastic Books.

    Katy and her brother Walter meet Marya, a Gypsy girl who is in town for the summer. After a rough start, the three become friends and Katy looks forward to Marya returning the next summer.

Yolen, J. (1988). *The devil's arithmetic*. New York: Viking, Penquin Books.

    Wondering why her Jewish family is constantly talking about the Holocaust, Hannah finds herself thrust back in time to the 1940s in a Polish shtetl and experiences the horror and fear of the death camps and Nazi atrocities.

STEREOTYPING, RACE, ETHNICITY, GENDER, AND EXCEPTIONALITIES

Bambara, T.C. (1992). *Gorilla my love*. New York: Vintage Books.
Fifteen stories of a wide range of characters in localities from uptown New York to rural North Carolina.

Bannerji, H. (1991). *Coloured pictures*. Toronto, Canada: Sister Vision.
Sujata, a 13-year-old South Asian, Canadian Sikh and her friends confront racism in her classroom and community.

Choi, S. N. (1991). *Year of impossible goodbyes*. New York: Houghton Mifflin.
Ten-year-old Sookan, a Korean, is caught in the Japanese and Russian occupation of North Korea during the 1940s. She later escapes to freedom in South Korea.

Cisneros, S. (1991). *House on Mango Street*. New York: Vintage Contemporaries.
Esperanza Cordero lives in a run-down Latino neighborhood in Chicago. She doesn't like the low expectations people have of her. It is the story of her coming of age and her survival, in spite of the odds against her.

Cofer, J. O. (1995). *An island like you: Stories of the barrio*. New York: Orchard Books.
Twelve stories describing how Puerto Rican young people experience growing up in Paterson, New Jersey.

Connolly, P. (1991). *Coaching Evelyn*. New York: HarperCollins.
Evelyn Ashford is a great American sprint champion. This book depicts many of the techniques and training regimen she used.

Crew, L. (1989). *Children of the river*. New York: Bantam
    Doubleday.

*Seventeen-year-old Sundara, an escapee from Cambodia and
the Khmer Rouge, must decide between her cultural traditions and
her new life in an Oregon high school.*

Flanigan, S. (1988). *Alice*. New York: St. Martin's Paperbacks.

*This book takes place deep in the Georgia mountains. A deaf
girl is taught to speak, read, and write by a young mountain girl.*

Fox, P. (1973). *The slave dancer*. New York: Laurel Leaf Books.

*Jessie was kidnapped to play music on the slave ship. The
owners wanted the slaves to "dance" to keep their muscles strong
and bring a better price when they were sold.*

Garfield, J.B. (1957). *Follow my leader*. New York: Apple Books,
    Scholastic

*Blinded in a firecracker accident, Jimmy has to re-learn
all the things he used to know. No matter how hard he has tried
in the past, he will need to try even harder to learn to work with
Leader his guide dog.*

George, J.C. (1972). *Julie of the wolves*. New York: HarperCollins.

*Thirteen-year-old Julie is running away from home and an
unwanted marriage, She learns to live in the wilderness with the
wolves as her companions.*

Gordon, S. (1987). *Waiting for the rain*. New York: Bantam
Books.

*Nine years in the life of two South African young men—one
white, one black, one who becomes a soldier, and one who becomes
a student, during the divisions caused by apartheid.*

Graf, N. (1993). *Where the river runs: A portrait of a refugee
    family*. Boston: Little.

*A Cambodian refugee family has to learn to adapt to their
new life in the United States.*

Gunn, P.A. (Ed.). (1989). *Spider Woman's granddaughters*. New York: Ballantine Books.
Spider Woman is credited in Cherokee legend as bringing the light of intelligence to her people.

Hesse, K. (1992), *Letters from Rifka,* NY: Puffin Books.
Rifka must remain in Belgium when her family flees from Russia in 1919. In her letters to her cousin, she relates all the experiences she is going through alone.

Jones, R. (1976). *The acorn people.* New York: Laurel Leaf Books.
Camp Wiggin is a special camp for physically disabled children. These children prove that physical disabilities cannot deter them from swimming and hiking. "The Acorn People" becomes their identifying logo.

Knight, M.B. (1993). *Who belongs here? An American story.* Gardiner, ME: Tilbury House.
Ten-year-old Nary has escaped from Cambodia and is both amazed and delighted at what he sees in America. His experiences in school with prejudice and bias somewhat dull these experiences.

Lawrence, J. (1993). *The great migration: An American story.* New York: HarperCollins.
Between 1916 and 1919, large groups of African Americans left their homes in the South for jobs and housing in the North. Northern workers were angry they had to compete for jobs with these immigrants.

Mochizuki, K. (1993). *Baseball saved us.* New York: Lee and Low.
During World War II when many Japanese and Japanese-Americans were interred, a young boy and his family build a baseball field. The young boy takes out his anger in a game-winning home run.

Mohr, N. (1986). *Felita*. New York: Dial Press.
This story of an eight-year-old Puerto Rican girl and her family as they discuss their everyday experiences living in a white, urban community.

Myers, W.D. (1989). *The young landlords*. New York: Puffin.
Five teenagers who have been friends for years, decide to make their Harlem neighborhood a better place to live.

O'Dell, S. (1990). *Island of the blue dolphin*. Boston: Houghton Mifflin.
A young Indian girl spends 18 years learning to survive and be happy on an isolated island off the coast of California. She learns she has a lot of courage and self-reliance.

Paterson K. (1978). *The great Gilly Hopkins*. New York: Crowell.
Eleven-year-old Gilly Hopkins is a foster child. To protect herself, she schemes against everyone who tries to help her. She does not dare let down her defenses for fear she will be hurt yet again.

Perkins, M. (1993). *The Sunita experiment*. Boston: Joy Street Books.
Thirteen-year-old Sunita is from India and living in California. When her Indian grandparents come for a visit she is embarrassed by their traditions and doesn't want her friends to be around them.

Polacco, P. (1994). *Pink and say*. New York: Philomel Books.
Patricia Polacco's great grandfather is one of the main characters in this picture book about a young white soldier and a young black soldier during the Civil War. The story shows the injustices, senselessness, and emotions surrounding those involved.

Ringgold, F. (1991). *Tar Beach*. New York: Crown Publishing.
Cassie Lightfoot has always wanted to fly. This story follows Cassie to the rooftop of the Harlem apartment building where her dream comes true.

Ross, R. B. (1992). *Bet's on, Lizzie Bingman.* New York: Houghton Mifflin.

In 1914, 14-year-old Lizzie bets with her oldest brother about women's suffrage. That summer finds her embroiled in many an adventure because of her bet.

Say, A. (1988). *A river dream.* New York: Houghton Mifflin.

A young boy opens a "special" box while he is sick in bed. What he finds helps him pursue a fantastic fishing trip with his uncle.

Say, A. (1993). *Grandfather's journey.* New York: Houghton Mifflin.

Grandfather loves to travel between his native Japan and California, wanting to be in Japan when he is in California and vice versa. His grandson has inherited his longing to travel and be where he isn't.

Spier, P. (1980). *People.* New York: Doubleday Books.

A delightful picture book expressing the richness of the differences among people around the world.

Spinelli, J. (1990). *Maniac Magee.* Boston: Little.

Twelve-year-old Jeffrey "Maniac" Magee is an orphan who travels to Two Mills, Pennsylvania, where he proves to be an unexpectedly accomplished athlete.

Taylor, M.D. (1973). *Song of the trees.* New York: Dial Books.

In the 1930s, in Mississippi, Cassie and her family try to save the forest on their land before an unscrupulous white man tries to destroy it.

Taylor, M.D. (1976). *Roll of thunder, hear my cry.* New York: Dial Books.

Cassie and her family try to understand the prejudice and discrimination they face as an African American family in a rural area.

Taylor, M.D. (1987). *The friendship*. New York: Dial Books.

In the 1930s, in Mississippi, Cassie and her brothers know they should not go near Wallace's store because he is a white man and it is dangerous. When they do go, they hear an old black man call Mr. Wallace by his first name, not the thing to do.

Taylor, M.D. (1990). *The road to Memphis*. New York: Dial Books.

Set in 1941 Mississippi. two white boys are teasing a young black boy who retaliates. He seeks Cassie's help to run away.

Thomasma. (1989). *Kuni: Escape on the Missouri*. Jackson, WY: Grandview.

An interesting account of an 1862 Sioux Indian uprising in Minnesota when the Sioux and Winnebago were forcibly removed from their land.

Turner, A. (1987). *Nettie's trip south*. New York: MacMillan.

A 10-year-old northern girl witnesses her first slave auction in 1859 when she visits family in Richmond, VA.

Walter, M. P. (1996). *Second daughter: The story of a slave girl*. New York: Scholastic.

Set in 1781, the true story of a slave girl who sued her owner for freedom under the Massachusetts constitution and won.

Yep, L. (1977). *Child of the owl*. New York: Harper.

Fearing a 12-year-old Chinese girl was forgetting her heritage, her family sends her to live with her grandmother in San Francisco's Chinatown.

Resources for Teaching Diversity

Delpit, L. (1995). *Other people's children: Cultural conflict in the classroom*. New York: The New Press.

Harris, V. (1992). *Teaching multicultural literature in grades K-8*. Norwood, MA: Christopher-Gordon Publishers.

King, J.E., Hollins, E.R., & Hayman, W.C. (1997). *Preparing teachers for cultural diversity*. New York: Teacher's College Press.

Ladson-Billings, G. (1994). *The dreamkeepers: Successful teachers of African American children*. San Francisco: Jossey-Bass.

Lee, E., Menkart, D., Okazawa-Rey, M. (Eds). (1998). *Beyond heroes and holidays: A practical guide to K-12 anti-racist, multicultural education and staff development*. Washington, DC: Network of Educators on the Americas.

Levine, M. (1993). *All kinds of minds: A young student's book about learning abilities and disabilities*. Cambridge, MA: Educator's Publishing Service.

Lowen, J. (1995). *Lies my teacher told me: Everything your American history textbook got wrong*. New York: New Press.

McConnell-Celi, S. (Ed.). (1993) *Twenty-first century challenge: Lesbians and gays in education bridging the gap*. Red Bank, NJ: Lavender Crystal Press.

Otero, E., & Smith, G. (1994). *Teaching about cultural awareness*. Denver, CO: Center for Teaching International Relations.

Sadkar, M., & Sadkar, D. (1994). *Failing at fairness: How America's schools cheat girls*. New York: MacMillan.

Schniedewind, N., & Davidson, E. (1998). *Open minds to equality: A sourcebook of learning activities to affirm diversity and promote equality* (2nd ed.). Needham Heights, MA: Longwood and Allyn & Bacon.

Sheppard, R.L., Rubel, K., Sheppard, K., Stratton, B., & Zigo, D. (2004). *Using literature to connect young adolescent concerns throughout the curriculum*. Westerville, OH: National Middle School Association.

Stein, N., & Sjostrom, L. (1994). *Flirting or hurting? A teacher's guide on sexual harassment in schools for 6th through 12th grade students.* Wellesley, MA: Wellesley College for Research on Women.

Wellesley College. Center for Research on Women., & American Association of University Women Educational Foundation. (1995). *How schools shortchange girls: The AAUW report: A study of major findings on girls and education.* New York: Marlowe.

Yarrow, Peter (2000). *Operation respect: Don't laugh at me.* New York and Cambridge, MA: Operation Respect and Education for Social Responsibility.

About the Author

Elizabeth Dore earned her undergraduate and two graduate degrees from the University of Maine and taught in Gardiner, Maine, for several years before heading to Colorado to earn her Ed.D. at the University of Northern Colorado in Greeley. She has been on the middle school faculty where she is associate professor at Radford University in Virginia since August 1996. Betty is editor of *The Crucial Link,* Virginia Middle School Association's newspaper, and in July 2004 will be installed as president of the association. She is the chair of the Virginia Schools to Watch Program and involved in several committees for National Middle School Association.